DESTINATION UNKNOWN

MISSIONS

30 Excursions to Transform Your Community

SAM HALVERSON

DESTINATION UNKNOWN

MISSIONS

30 EXCURSIONS TO TRANSFORM YOUR COMMUNITY

SAM HALVERSON

DESTINATION UNKNOWN MISSIONS
30 EXCURSIONS TO TRANSFORM YOUR COMMUNITY

ISBN 9781426753794

12 13 14 15 16 17 18 19 20 21 — 10 9 8 7 6 5 4 3 2 1

MANUFACTURED IN THE UNITED STATES OF AMERICA

TABLE OF CONTENTS

*Permission is granted to photocopy these forms for groups using *Destination Unknown Missions.* ©2012 Abingdon Press.

ADVENTURE

INTRODUCTION

MYSTERY TRIPS?

The previous DESTINATION UNKNOWN books were named such because they contained a collection of mystery trips. The idea behind a mystery trip is that the youth have no idea where they are going until they get there.

This book is a little bit different. Some of the destinations in this book will work as mystery trips; and some work best as mystery trips. But, for others, it may be helpful to tell youth in advance where they will be going and what they will be doing. And there may be situations where it is more interesting to say, "We're going someplace where you'll experience John 13:34 a little better," than to say, "We're going to the corner gas station to wash car windows."

Perhaps the real "unknown" about these destinations is where they will take youth spiritually, over the long-term. The point of this book is not to provide youth with a one-time experience, but to introduce them to organizations, activities, and ministries that can offer them avenues of service for months and years to come.

Through each of the activities in DESTINATION UNKNOWN MISSIONS youth will make an impact on their community, and they will become aware of needs in their community. Along the way they will meet Jesus, serve Jesus, work with Jesus, and show Jesus to others as they spend time with persons who are homeless, hungry, or strangers.

Many of these destinations work well as a part of your evening youth fellowship programming, though some would be difficult on Sunday evenings, when the businesses or agencies involved may be closed. Others will require more planning and preparation and may be better suited for a Saturday afternoon. In some cases (such as for the "Awareness Walk"), the initial destination involves meeting to plan something you'll actually do later.

In addition to short-term destinations, this book also includes suggestions for a day camp for children and a weeklong mission camp for youth. Both of these activities give your congregation an opportunity to reach out to young people in your community.

Those of us in youth ministry have a responsibility to involve teens in doing the work of mercy and justice that God calls all Christians to do. We often do this by taking youth on mission trips to other parts of the country or world. We spend our time on these excursions telling them that Christ wants to them to serve. But when they return home, they don't know where to begin. If they feel called to work with people who are homeless, where do they start? If they are passionate about making sure that all people have access to food, whom should they call?

Notes

Destination Unknown Missions 30 Excursions to Transform Your Community

If their skills lie in home repair, how can they put these skills to use? These destinations will connect your youth to local service agencies and introduce your youth to a variety of ways they can use their gifts to show people in your community God's love and blessings.

To make the most out of these destinations, you will need to make connections to Scripture and to the youths' experiences. To help you do this, each destination in this book includes the following:

Scripture

Each program has at least one key Scripture. Read and reflect on this Scripture as you prepare for the destination. Assign one or two youth to be the Scripture readers for each activity.

About the Destination

This section gives a little information about the site and how to prepare for the visit. Read this material early in your planning, as there are resource suggestions and background work you may need to accomplish ahead of time. Also, review this information a day or so before the activity.

Bright Idea

Each program includes at least one Bright Idea. These are added suggestions that will allow you and your group to make this experience, or a future experience, even more meaningful.

On the Way

If you're meeting at one central location and then traveling as a group to your site, then this section is for you. The discussion questions included don't usually give away the destination, but they help prepare youth for the experience in a simple, non-threatening way.

At the Site

This section provides the "meat" of the program. Read and study these steps while you're planning and make any changes needed to suit your group.

PROMOTE AND COMMUNICATE

It is important that you promote each destination in ways that will catch the youths' attention and keep them interested. The best way to do this is to give them a little hint about where you'll be going—just enough to pique their curiosity. The key Scripture for a destination is a good hint to use. In an e-mail or text or in the church bulletin the week prior, you could write: *"Next Sunday at 7:00 P.M. the youth group will meet at the church and travel to a Destination Unknown. The destination is secret, but read John 6:26-51 for a clue."* Have fun with these programs and help the youth recognize ways that God calls them to live lives of mission and service right in their own community.

Notes

ADVENTURE

Another great way to promote your Destination Unknown is to mail cards that include a map to the location and a time for youth to meet you there. This works great for small groups and removes problems associated with transportation. However, if you choose this option, you will need to use the "On the Way" section of each program at another time. Some of those can be finished by the youth themselves on their way to the meeting (if you put the instructions in the mailing); others will need to be discussed as soon as the youth arrive.

Remember to communicate to the parents of your youth the time you expect to return from the destination. Each destination is different. Some may take only an hour, while others may take an entire afternoon or day. Just because you returned before dinner on one occasion doesn't mean it will be the same time the next week.

Plan for Safe Transportation

You will need to make sure that you have enough drivers and appropriate transportation for each excursion. Always plan for more youth than you expect. It's easier to tell volunteers that you don't need them to drive than to tell a youth that there is no room for him or her to come along.

Also, it's important to remember that any time you travel with your youth, they should not be allowed to drive. The only exception is if a youth has parental permission to drive alone. Allowing youth to drive only invites complications and places too much responsibility on them.

Try to avoid situations where an adult is alone in a car with youth. It is best to have two unrelated adults in any vehicle. For this reason, large vehicles (with, say, two adults and five youth) are better than smaller vehicles.

This same principle applies once you reach your destination. Avoid situations where an individual adult is alone with youth. Such situations leave both the youth and the adult vulnerable to abuse or allegations of abuse. If your church has safety policies for adults working with youth, be sure to follow them.

Notes

ADOPT A CHILD

FOCUS

Youth will take needy children, whose names will be provided by a social agency or community center, shopping for Christmas gifts that they can wrap and give to family members, helping those children experience the joy of giving as well as the compassion of Christ.

SCRIPTURE

Acts 20:35

LOCATION

A shopping center and a local agency or community center that reaches out to children of needy families

ABOUT THE DESTINATION

We have often heard the quote, "It is more blessed to give than to receive," but if we truly believe that, then why don't we spend more time and money helping people experience this blessing of "giving"? There are many children living in poverty who can be blessed on Christmas Day by watching loved ones open gifts that the children picked out, wrapped, and gave out of love. Your youth can be a part of giving that blessing to those children.

For this destination you will need to contact a local children's home, a community center frequented by children from needy families, or a social agency that serves low-income families. It is better to work through one of these organizations than to compile your own list of families, as you are establishing a relationship with a local agency where your youth can volunteer in the months and years ahead. Explain to the organization's representatives what you want to do and ask them to help with some of the legwork, if possible:

- ✪ Ask for a list of children's names who will be attending. (Limit their ages to a manageable range, like 4 to fourth grade. You should receive this list at least a week in advance so that you can make sure you have enough youth and money.)

Preparation

- ✪ Contact a children's home, community center, or social agency and ask to take some children Christmas shopping. Also ask for family members' names for each child.

- ✪ Ask the center or agency to collect permission forms and contact information for each child participating and to send along one adult volunteer.

- ✪ Prepare a flier to send home with children (see page 10).

- ✪ Prepare one envelope per participating child and place money inside. (see page 10).

- ✪ Review Acts 20:35.

Bright Ideas

❂ Consider doing a two-week carryover between this destination and the Santa's Day Out destination (see page 95). Invite the same children to both activities.

❂ With some planning and foresight you can include this outreach in the budget for each ministry year. Another funding option is to ask for donations from the congregation. A third option is to ask each youth who participates to donate a specified amount. This actually allows the youth first to experience "giving," then to see the money they give being used in ministry. If you choose this option, though, emphasize from the perspective of a serving opportunity.

❂ Ask for a list of family members for each child (parents, siblings, grandparents) who live in the same home. These will be the people for whom youth and the children will buy gifts.

❂ Prior to the event ask the organization to gather permission forms and emergency contact information from the parents of the children attending.

❂ Ask the organization to send along at least one adult volunteer. The parents of the children will feel more comfortable about sending their children with you if they recognize a familiar face.

Once you receive a list of children and the household members for whom they will be buying gifts, collect the money to spend on the gifts. Divide the total amount of money in your budget by the number of gifts you need to purchase. Prepare an envelope for each child, with that child's name written on the envelope, as well as the names and ages of those for whom the child will be purchasing gifts, and place enough cash in the envelope for each gift to be purchased.

Finally, locate a shopping area that is either enclosed (like a mall) or stands mostly alone. It is important that your youth (who will work in pairs or threesomes with a child) can keep track of the child entrusted to them. Talk with the staff of the shopping area where you will be taking the children and ask if any stores will give discounts or donations for the program. Ask if there is a place where the children may wrap their gifts before you take them back to meet their parents. Also ask if any stores will donate wrapping paper and tape. You should arrange transportation plans, too—either providing enough vans or buses for all the children and youth or asking the cooperating organization if they can transport the children and meet you at the shopping area.

Make sure the parents know when their children will return, and create a small flier to give the parents which reads (see page 127 for photocopiable text):

Thank you for allowing us to spend time with your child today. A big part of the Christmas blessing is being able to experience it through the excitement of children, and in this you have given us a blessing. We took your child shopping to purchase gifts for your family so that he or she can give gifts to family members on Christmas Day. Please try not to open these gifts until the day that you open your other Christmas gifts, since a part of the gift your child receives is the opportunity to give a gift to everyone else. Thanks again, and may you and your family truly experience God's gift that is Christmas!

ON THE WAY

As you and the youth travel to pick up or meet the children, ask youth about some of the best and most memorable gifts they have ever received: What made these gifts special? Did they ever receive anonymous gifts or gifts from a stranger? What did they think about that experience? What can make a gift special if it is received from a stranger? Also talk about the joy of giving gifts. Ask the youth to tell about special gifts they have given. Were they ever disappointed in the response from the person who received the gift? What kind of responses do they expect today from the children who will be buying their gifts to give others? What kind of responses do they expect from the parents when they learn about the gifts purchased?

AT THE SITE

1. Before the children arrive, pair up youth and give each pair an envelope labeled with a child's name, along with the names of gift recipients, and money inside.

2. Greet the children and make a special effort to meet each parent, thanking them for the time you can spend with their children and explaining what you will be doing. Make sure they hear the time you will be returning with the children.

3. Before pairs, adults, and children begin shopping, remind youth that their biggest responsibility is to keep the children in their care safe. Communicate the time when the youth and children should return to wrap the gifts, along with a cell phone number where you or another adult can be reached. (At least two adults should not be attached to children in case there is a situation in which an adult is needed immediately.)

   Also instruct the youth pairs to keep all receipts and place them in the envelopes as they make their purchases. Explain that the receipts and the leftover cash, if any, should total the original amount of money they received.

   Some youth will ask if they can purchase gifts for the children with whom they are shopping. This is up to you and your group, but make sure that the main focus is on the gifts the children will buy and give—not on what the children might receive individually. The children should not get the idea that they are giving "in order to get" something.

4. When the youth and children return from shopping to wrap their gifts, talk about the shopping experience and what kinds of gifts the children purchased. Ask the children if they think their parents and brothers and sisters will be happy to receive the gifts. While they wrap their gifts and place name tags on each one, ask some of your youth to tell the Christmas story to the children.

5. When everyone has finished wrapping gifts, sing a few Christmas carols, if possible. Then gather the gifts and the children and return to meet their parents. Thank the parents and make sure that the appropriate gifts and the flier explaining the purpose of your day accompanies each child.

Notes

Adopt a Child

ADVENTURE

6. When all the children are gone, talk with your youth about today's experience of serving. Ask the youth to tell about their shopping time, the celebrations as well as the frustrations. Talk about the following:

- ❂ How could you make this experience better next time?
- ❂ In what ways were youth's expectations met?
- ❂ How were their expectations exceeded?
- ❂ How were their expectations not met?
- ❂ How did the youth experience giving?
- ❂ How were they blessed by giving today?

7. Close in prayer, asking each youth to name aloud the child he or she helped to buy Christmas gifts.

Notes

Help the children and your youth experience the joy of
giving and the compassion of Christ.

ADOPT A HIGHWAY

FOCUS

Youth will spend time along a nearby highway picking up trash and finding other ways to beautify the roadway, while focusing on how God works through us to make an impact on our community.

SCRIPTURE

Nehemiah 3:1-5

LOCATION

A section of a nearby highway

ABOUT THE DESTINATION

Every state department of transportation has an "Adopt-A-Highway" program through which a group can request a certain section of a local highway and commit to keeping that area clean. Groups often have the option of posting a sign that alerts others who is responsible for keeping the stretch of highway clean and maintained.

Before deciding whether your youth would like to take on this responsibility, meaning that your group would commit to cleaning and beautifying that section of highway a number of times throughout the year, you should ask if your church already has made such a commitment. Sometimes a group adopts a section of highway and then, over the years, forgets about the commitment.

If you do not wish to commit to the actual Adopt-A-Highway program, your group can still take on the task for a single act of service, making an impact on the community and saving the highway department the cost of such care. Contact your department of transportation and ask for suggested areas or, if you have an area in mind, ask if someone is already responsible for it. If not, inform the DOT of where and when you and your group plan on working.

Read the Scripture ahead of time, practicing the pronunciation of the names in the text. Stumbling over words will only detract from the significance of all the people who helped in the Hebrews' building of the wall.

Preparation

✪ Find out if your congregation previously adopted a stretch of roadside through your state's Adopt-A-Highway program. If not, sign up now.

✪ Provide garbage bags and a brightly colored vest or shirt for each participant (if the department of transporation does not do so). Also provide drinking water.

✪ Remind youth to bring work gloves.

✪ Review Nehemiah 3:1-5 and practice pronunciation.

The department of transportation often provides vests and garbage bags for volunteers. Check to see if they will do so; if not, provide garbage bags, drinking water, and some type of brightly colored vests or shirts. Also be sure to communicate ahead of time that participants should bring gloves to wear while working.

On the Way

Talk with the youth about various community service jobs. Ask them to call out some examples. Which jobs do they notice the most? Why? What are some ways of serving in the community that appeal to them? Which kinds of community service would they never want to do? Why? Do they think some tasks are beneath them (not good enough for them to do)? Why or why not?

At the Site

Bright Ideas

♻ Take the opportunity to invite another group in your church to join you on this service outing. Sharing in service helps people of different ages, or with different interests, to bond. Integrated service helps the body of Christ grow closer together.

1. Drive the adopted stretch of roadway with your youth. Casually point out some of the trash you notice along the roadside as you approach where the group will work, saying something like: "Why do people just throw out their junk? How hard is it for folks to keep their trash until they can put it in a trash can?" Finally, stop the car and explain that you will serve where you see the need: right here.

2. Before actually beginning the work, gather everyone together and give some background information about Nehemiah. Explain that many of the people of Judah had been refugees in Babylon, taken after Babylon defeated them several decades earlier. The exiles, upon returning to their homeland, discovered their beloved city of Jerusalem was still in shambles. Nehemiah, a Jewish exile who had served as the cupbearer to the king of Babylon, realized it was his calling to organize, motivate, and lead in the rebuilding of the wall around Jerusalem. Rebuilding this wall was a matter of national security and not simply a beautification project. Everyone stepped up and served in the task. Everyone, that is, except for one family.

3. Now read aloud Nehemiah 3:1-5. Explain that even after verse 5 (where we learn that the nobles of the Tekoites refused to do the work), the Scripture continues naming all the families who helped rebuild the entire wall that circled the city of Jerusalem. Everyone present participated in the work—except the Tekoite nobles. They were lazy or thought themselves too important to do such menial labor. The result of believing themselves too good for such work, though, is that the Tekoites are forever noted in Scripture as the only family who did not work on the wall. The Bible never mentions them again.

4. Ask: "Why is it important to work together on tasks that help the community around us? What do you gain from such work? How does the community benefit? Why shouldn't we just let someone else do it?" Explain that your work today, in addition to making the roadside look nicer, will save the county or the state from having to pay someone else to do the work, allowing those funds to be spent on other important projects that also help the community.

5. Try to keep the group together as you begin the work, keeping participants safe along the highway and allowing them to bond. Make sure that someone is assigned to watch and call out when cars are coming, if you are working on a road that isn't very busy. However, if it is a busy road, remind workers to be continaully mindful of the heavy traffic.

6. As participants work, take some pictures and show them in church the following Sunday or post them on the church website. You also might consider taking before-and-after pictures.

7. When the stretch of roadway is clean, say a prayer over the work you have accomplished and thank God for the opportunity to serve in your community.

Help your youth focus on how God works through
us to make an impact on our community.

Notes

ANIMAL SHELTER

FOCUS

Youth will visit a local animal shelter and volunteer to clean, help with other needed tasks, and spend time with the animals. They will focus on our calling and responsibility to care for all of God's creation.

SCRIPTURE

Genesis 1:28-31; Psalm 24:1

LOCATION

The local animal shelter or Humane Society

ABOUT THE DESTINATION

Most shelters have more than enough animals. They are always looking for households to adopt pets. While you shouldn't expect all of your youth and their families to adopt a cat or dog, this destination is a good way to teach them about the work of the local shelter and how they can volunteer.

Contact your local shelter and explain that you would like to bring your group to help clean and play with the animals. Ask for convenient dates and times and also arrange for a tour of the facility.

Review the Scriptures before talking with youth about God's call for us to care for animals.

Remind youth to wear appropriate clothes and shoes for working at the site.

ON THE WAY

As you travel to the destination, ask the youth about the different pets they have owned and cared for during their lives. What did they like about those pets? What sort of responsibilities did they have for their pets? Do they think God intended for some animals to be treated as pets?

Preparation

❂ Contact an area animal shelter and arrange a time when your group can tour and help clean and do other tasks.

❂ Review Genesis 1:28-31 and Psalm 24:1.

AT THE SITE

1. Before going inside the shelter, read aloud Genesis 1:28-31 and Psalm 24:1. Then ask:

   - The entire world belongs to God and was created by God. Why should we care for God's creation? Why not just let God care for the world?
   - What does it mean to have responsibility for something?
   - How can we have authority over the animals but also be responsible for their well-being?
   - What mistakes has our society made with the animal population?

2. Introduce the youth to the tour guide (if applicable) and other personnel at the shelter. Learn all you can about the work of the shelter. Encourage the youth to ask questions and be prepared to ask some questions of your own.

3. Listen as the guide explains some of the jobs that the youth will do to help. Then divide the group into work teams and begin.

4. Encourage the youth as they work, pointing out that both the animals and the people who work at the shelter benefit from their help. The animals benefit because the workers will be in a much better mood as a result of the help they are receiving. And the workers benefit from having fewer tasks to accomplish.

5. When the work is finished and everyone who could has spent some time with the animals, gather the group together and reread Genesis 1:28-31 and Psalm 24:1. Ask:

   - What does it mean to "take charge" of all the animals? What responsibilities does this involve?
   - What does it mean for "the earth . . . and everything in it" to belong to God? What does this phrase mean for how we treat animals?

   Ask the group to define the word *steward*. If no one offers a proper definition, explain that a *steward* is someone who has been given authority to care for property by the owner of that property. Ask:

   - As stewards of God's creation, what kinds of responsibilities do we have?

6. As you prepare to leave the shelter, thank the workers and say a closing prayer for the group, thanking God for animals and asking God to watch over those who care for the animals. Also ask God to guide your community toward being responsible for the care and treatment of animals like these.

Bright Ideas

- Many shelters have a schedule for volunteers to come and help clean the facility or to simply spend time with the animals. Encourage your youth to consider volunteering once a month or a quarter to help in the shelter.

Destination Unknown Missions 30 Excursions to Transform Your Community

Awareness Walk

Focus

Youth will plan and organize a walk to educate the public (children, youth, and adults) about the reality of homelessness and poverty in their area and to generate financial support for a local ministry that serves the homeless population.

Scripture

John 1:14

Location

A walk route in an area of your community where homeless persons spend a lot of time

About the Destination

This destination will require a lot of planning and organizing, but it has the potential to draw the community together in ministry and outreach. Enlist the members of your congregation and local businesses in the planning and support of this event.

The walk is more than simply a long hike through town. In fact, consider organizing several walks so that participants may choose which one they wish to experience. Each walk should give participants a firsthand look at poverty and homelessness. The money raised should be used to assist a local agency or ministry that reaches out to the homeless or those struggling with poverty.

Before meeting with your youth to plan this event, consider inviting some representatives of agencies that serve the poor and homeless in your community. Also work with one of these agencies to invite one or more of the persons they serve or have served. Be careful not to be patronizing or condescending toward your homeless or formerly homeless guest(s); you don't want him or her to feel self-conscious. The insight and testimony of these guests will be valuable as you go forward in planning this destination.

When you first meet with the youth to plan this event, gather at the church. Conduct later meetings along the walk route.

Preparation

✪ Locate an area in your community where many homeless persons live and spend their time.

✪ Schedule a planning meeting and use the instructions and suggestions on pages 20-21.

✪ Invite guests from local agencies that serve the homeless population to participate in the planning. Also enlist help in contacting a homeless or formerly homeless guest(s) to give insight to the planning.

✪ Review John 1:14.

ADVENTURE

For more ideas research similar events on the Internet, such as The Walk for the Homeless which is sponsored by Good Works, Inc. each year in Athens, Ohio (see *www.walkforthehomeless.net*).

On the Way

As youth arrive at the church to plan the event, talk about what they think it would be like to be homeless: How would they wash their clothes? Where would they eat? Where would they sleep?

At the Site

Bright Ideas

IDEA

❂ Though it could be uncomfortable, consider holding this event during the winter if you live in a colder climate. Your purpose is to help people understand the struggles of the poor and homeless. What better way to learn about these struggles than to observe how the homeless search for warmth in the cold of winter.

❂ This is an experience that people will want you to offer every year. As you organize this event, look for people from your church's outreach or missions committee to help. Delegate jobs so that this can become an annual event.

1. Explain to the youth that it is difficult to relate to the plight of the homeless in our community when we haven't walked in their shoes. Tell the group about the event they will plan. Ask, "Why do we separate ourselves from the homeless and poor?"

2. Read aloud John 1:14. This is a Scripture about God (the Word) who "moved into the neighborhood" (as Eugene Peterson states in *THE MESSAGE*) in the person of Jesus. Explain that, just as God decided to be present with us and experience life with us, so we are called to be present with others in their lives. Ask:

 ❂ How did Jesus become "present" with those whom he encountered?
 ❂ How can being present with homeless people in our community help them to experience Christ?

3. Introduce the youth to any guests. Then begin the business of planning. Here is what you and your group will need to decide:

 ❂ How much money should each walker donate? Registered walkers should be encouraged to enlist sponsors. You could ask each walker to enlist ten sponsors who will pledge $10 each, meaning each person donates $100 for the walk.

 ❂ Who will sponsor this event? You will need people to donate food, signs, advertising, T-shirts, and any supplies or printed materials needed for the walk.

 ❂ How long should the walks be and where should they go? None of the walks need to be long. The important thing is what people learn and experience along the way.

 ❂ Where should the walks begin? Locate a church or parking lot to serve as a starting and finishing point in the area where the walks will take place.

✪ <u>Who else will be involved?</u> Plan on inviting other churches in the community to promote and participate in this event. It will be successful only if the whole community is involved and not just your church.

✪ <u>What will be the schedule for the walk?</u> Plan for registration to begin about a half hour before the walk begins. Also allow for some time to welcome people and to explain the various routes. Conclude with a lunch of bread, rice, and beans while participants talk about their experiences.

✪ <u>What will happen on the walks?</u> How will each walk be unique? What do people need to learn about those living in poverty? Allow your group to think of creative ways to educate the walkers about issues of addiction and drugs, education, abuse, children growing up in poverty, and what it's like to live on the streets.

✪ <u>What are other ways to promote the walk?</u> T-shirts are a great way to promote (and help people remember) the event. Designate someone to be in charge of designing and purchasing the shirts.

4. Determine the times and places for your follow-up planning meetings. Hold these meeting along the walk routes. Designate someone to contact the team, sending out reminders about the meetings and tasks to be completed between meetings.

5. Close the meeting with prayer, asking God to guide everyone in the planning and execution of this event.

Notes

It is difficult to relate to the plight of the homeless in our community when we haven't walked in their shoes.

BACK TO SCHOOL

FOCUS

Youth will organize and carry out a back-to-school program, offering local students every possible advantage as they begin the new school year.

SCRIPTURE

Acts 4:32-37; Philippians 4:19

LOCATION

A local church setting in the community that is near where children live who need back-to-school help and support

ABOUT THE DESTINATION

When summer is winding down and a new school year is approaching, many families will be busy shopping for all the clothes and supplies their children need for school. Some families have no trouble buying everything they need, but others are not so fortunate. These families may not be able to afford new backpacks and school supplies, let alone new clothes. Involve your youth in helping children who need assistance with their back-to-school supplies and preparation.

Finding a location for the event is the first step. Research the area to locate a church or public community building that is in close proximity to the families who most need this help. Also notify other local churches and invite them to participate in the event and inform the families they know who need help. Contact churches that have vans or buses, along with certified drivers who will be able to pick up families and transport them to the event.

Enlist a team of youth to plan and organize this outreach. Also involve people serving on your local church missions team or council. If a similar ministry is already in place in your church or community, find a way that your youth can participate or take responsiblity for a part of it. Hold your first planning meeting in the location you choose for the event.

As you plan for the event, answer the questions on the following page:

As you plan for the event, answer the questions on the following page:

Preparation

- ✪ Determine a time and place to provide back-to-school items to community children.

- ✪ Contact the public schools in your area and obtain supply lists for students. Distribute to church members or post on church website.

- ✪ Contact other churches and businesses and agencies in your community about contributing items and/or services.

- ✪ Plan to provide thank-you cards for all those who donate supplies and services.

- ✪ Review Acts 4:32-37 and Philippians 4:19.

Bright Ideas

IDEA

- ⚙ This outreach project can make a huge impact on your community. If a ministry such as this is not available, talk with church leaders to determine if a group would be willing to organize an annual event like this one.

- ⚙ Some high schools require that seniors complete a service project in order to graduate. This would make a great senior project because it must occur early in the school year and would be completed before homework and other projects begin.

⚙ What will you call this event?

⚙ When will you schedule the event (date and time)?

⚙ What grade levels will it serve?

⚙ How will you organize the event?

⚙ Will you need to provide transportation for families?

⚙ What types of supplies and services will you offer? Here are some possibilities:

—Backpacks filled with pencils, notebooks, and other supplies

—Haircuts or gift certificates for haircuts

—Socks and underwear

—Medical screenings

Plan to set up several different stations (such as boys clothing, girls clothing, school supplies for kindergarten, school supplies for first grade, and so on). Assign volunteers to work at each station, greeting families and managing supply inventory. Also enlist a few adult volunteers to continually walk through the space and be available for any unexpected needs or information.

Most of the items or services can be donated or offered by volunteers. At least two months prior to the event, contact the public schools in your area and obtain official supply lists for students, then distribute these lists to your congregation (or post on a website, if possible). Contact an area hair salon and ask if there are stylists willing to donate their time and expertise to give haircuts on that day. Also contact a county health clinic about providing free medical screenings.

Contact local news agencies and enlist their help in promoting the event ahead of time. Also request a photographer and reporter to attend the event and write a follow-up story.

ON THE WAY

Talk with youth about their memories of the first days of school. When they were younger, what did they look forward to when preparing for a new school year? What was exciting about it? What did they dread?

AT THE SITE

1. As the youth plan the event, nurture excitement by talking about the impact God can have through the work you are doing. Read aloud Acts 4:32-37, then talk about how the early church recognized and met people's needs. God used the community of faith to be God's arms and hands, reaching out into hurting communities. God continues to work through God's people today. As they plan and carry out this event, God will use them to have an effect on children, their families, and even other volunteers.

2. Help the youth work out the details for the event using the questions on page 24. Determine who will be in charge of reaching out to donors and contacting local agencies and businesses that could offer help and support. (An adult may need to contact a county health clinic if you plan to offer medical screenings.) Involve as many youth as possible in the planning and preparation.

3. Schedule future meetings to check on progress and talk about issues as they arise. Also make plans to update the members of your congregation on the event and ways they can help.

4. On the day of the event, ask youth and other volunteers to come early and spend time in prayer before the children and their families begin to arrive.

5. During the event, make sure the preenlisted youth volunteers are at every station to greet families and manage inventory. And remind adult volunteers to walk around the space providing a visual reminder of additional help, if necessary.

6. When the event is over, gather together all volunteers for a time of prayer. Ask God for continued guidance in meeting the needs of students in your community and for blessings on all the families who participated. Thank everyone involved and provide thank-you cards for volunteers to sign, then mail the cartds to all those who donated services and items.

7. Close by reading aloud Philippians 4:19.

Notes

....
God uses the community of faith to be God's arms and hands.
....

CHILDREN'S CARNIVAL

FOCUS

Youth will organize, advertise, and host a free carnival for area children and their families.

SCRIPTURES

Matthew 18:3; 19:14; Mark 9:33-37

LOCATION

An area parking lot or playground

ABOUT THE DESTINATION

This carnival will require planning and preparation, but it will be a lot of fun and can have a positive impact on your community. Unlike many of the other destinations offered in this book, this one will not be a secret. Present this idea to your youth and allow them to plan the entire carnival with your guidance. Before you meet with the youth, though, research areas of your community where such a carnival could take place. Even though your church may be a workable location, think first about whether hosting the event at your church will communicate that this carnival is only for the children in your congregation. Local parks or school yards are neutral territories that allow for community outreach.

ON THE WAY

As youth arrive at the church (if you're holding the carnival there), or as you travel to the carnival location, ask them to recall what they used to do in their neighborhoods on a Saturday. Do they remember participating in community activities? If so, what? What kinds of things draw together a community? How can the church be a vital presence in the community and for its members? Why is this important?

Preparation

- Locate a space to hold the carnival, preferably an elementary school or park.

- Decide games and activities and enlist youth volunteers to prepare and oversee these.

- Purchase prizes; enlist someone to design a promotional flier.

- Secure a sound system, enlist a photographer, and ask church members to transport supplies and materials.

- Prepare photography release forms (see page 127).

- Review Matthew 18:3; 19:14; Mark 9:33-37.

AT THE SITE

1. Begin at your church—or park or other location where the carnival will be held. Present the task of planning and running the carnival. Explain to the youth your vision of what can happen and then read aloud the Scriptures. Talk about Mark 9:33-37 for a few minutes, then ask:

- ❂ What were the disciples talking about?
- ❂ What is the lesson that Jesus was trying to teach his followers?
- ❂ Why did Jesus call for a child to communicate this lesson?
- ❂ What is it about the kingdom of God that we can communicate to children and their families through this carnival?

2. Involve the youth in as much planning and in as many tasks as possible. Use the following checklist:

- ❂ <u>Find a location</u>. A local parking lot or playground works best. It should be within walking distance of the children you will invite. Contact a local elementary school or the city parks department for permission to use its facilities. Choose a location that has access to water, toilet facilities, and a nearby source of electricity.
- ❂ <u>Determine a day and time for the carnival</u>. A Saturday is ideal, but consider other local events such as parades or recreational activities. Choose a day and time when parents and other family members can join their children.
- ❂ <u>Decide on activities and games</u>. A carnival is all about fun and community connections. Think of it as a huge neighborhood party with enough game opportunities and activities that children won't have to wait long to participate. A ring toss, corn-hole game, pie-in-the-face game, and fishing-pond game are all easy and inexpensive to set up. (But you will have to find volunteers, whether youth or adults, who are willing to get hit in the face with pies.) Other games may be more complicated, but the diversity of activities will add to the fun. Try to find a dunk tank, a bounce house, or offer a cakewalk. Face painting is also easy to do and fun for the children. Finally, organize a closing talent show to bring everyone together for some entertainment and memory-making fun.
- ❂ <u>Locate and contact sources for small prizes</u>. You may need to spend a little money on this one, but don't go for expensive or big.
- ❂ <u>Get the word out</u>. Enlist someone to create fliers to deliver to neighborhood houses a day or two prior to the event. Print the location, date, and time on the fliers as well as the words "Free Carnival." Ask someone in your church who has a computer to design the flier.
- ❂ <u>Enlist volunteers</u> from your congregation if you need more people to help oversee the booths and games.

Bright Ideas
IDEA

- ❂ Think about inviting other area youth groups to participate in planning and running the carnival.

- ❂ Show the children and their families that this carnival isn't a ploy to get them inside a church, but is meant to show area children that they are loved and that Christ is present in their community.

- ☺ Secure a sound system. While a hand-held electric megaphone will amplify a voice to people nearby, a sound system will project farther and will allow you to play music throughout the event.
- ☺ If possible, enlist someone to take pictures at the event (someone fron your church is fine). Prepare release forms (see below) to hand out and to inform people that you'll be showing the pictures—with their approval—at worship on the following Sunday. Also include an invitation, with date and time, for them to attend that Sunday celebration. Minors (under age 18) will need to have their parents sign the approval forms on their behalf. Forms can include simple permission statements with the person's or child's name, date of use for the picture, and a signature (see page 127).

3. Conclude the planning meeting by scheduling a follow-up meeting and making sure everyone has agreed to complete at least one task before the next meeting. Collect contact information, if necessary, so you can follow up on assigned preparations. Close with a prayer that God will use the event to show the children and their families that they are loved and cherished members of the community.

4. Contact everyone on the planning team prior to follow-up meetings. Remind them of the next meeting and to complete all advance preparations.

5. At the follow-up meeting, connect any loose ends and finalize plans (transportation of materials and supplies, construction of props, a back-up plan for inclement weather, and cleanup). Close with a prayer of blessing for all who attend and participate.

6. On the day of the event, offer lots of encouragement and praise to those who did the planning and preparation. If you enlisted a photographer, remember to hand out the release forms you prepared ahead of time.

7. When the carnival is over, assemble the youth who participated and ask for feedback. Evaluate what worked and what didn't. Consider if you should do this type ministry again and what you would change if you did. Read aloud Matthew 18:3 and 19:14 to the group. Ask, "What is it about the children you saw today that reminds you of the kingdom of heaven?" Remind the youth to speak and be friendly when they see, in the neighborhood or at church, the families and children they met today. Thank everyone involved and close with a prayer, thanking God for this opportunity to experience the fun and excitement of children.

Notes

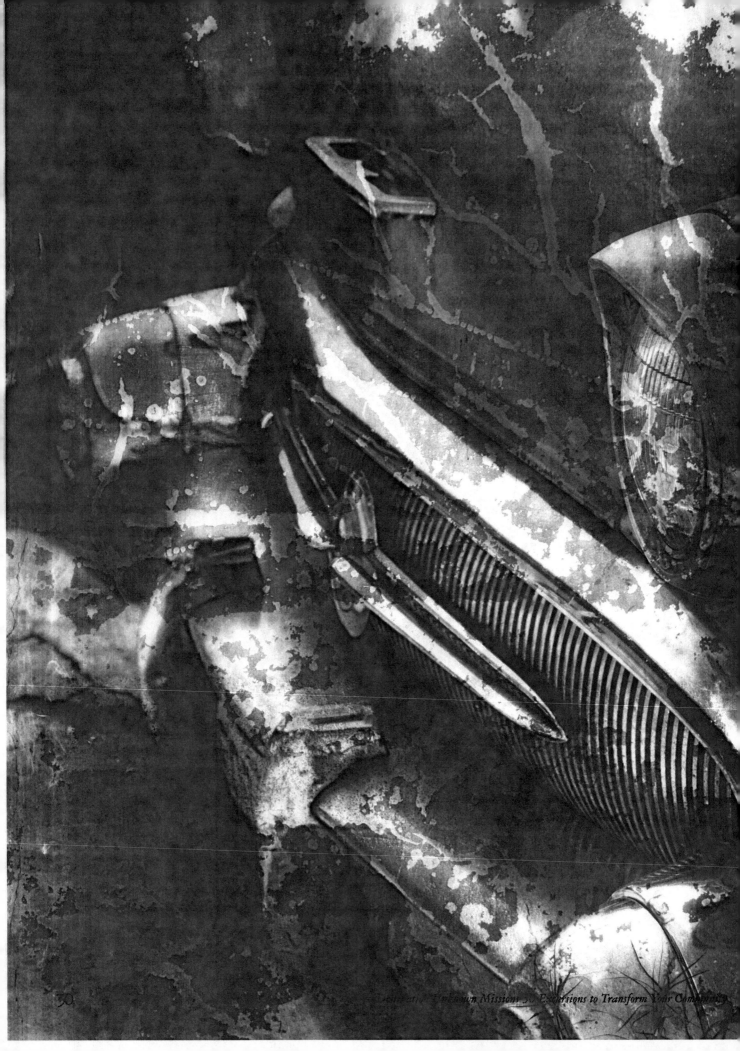

Celebrating Unknown Missions: 30 Excursions to Transform Your Community

CHRISTMAS CAROLING

FOCUS

Youth will visit homebound and church staff or neighborhoods near the church, singing Christmas carols and spreading Christmas blessings.

SCRIPTURE

1 Thessalonians 5:11-12

LOCATION

Nearby neighborhoods and homes

ABOUT THE DESTINATION

Spread some joy during pre-Christmas preparations by taking your group to nearby homes for Christmas caroling. This is best scheduled for an evening when most people are likely to be home. Talk with a pastor to find out who could use some Christmas joy and make a list of homes for youth to visit, along with directions.

If you have a large group of youth, or a large number of houses that need to be visited, divide the youth into smaller caroling groups, give each a list with directions to the homes, and assign a few adults to accompany each group.

ON THE WAY

Ask the group to name their favorite Christmas carols. If the drive to the destination takes a while, play "Call the Carol." Here's how you play:

- First, turn the radio to a station that plays only Christmas carols.
- Tell the group that they can earn points by guessing the next carol to be played. If they guess correctly, they get three points. If the next song played is the song they previously guessed, then they get one point.
- For example: Bill guesses "Joy to the World" and Tonya guesses "Sleigh Ride," while another carol is being played. When the next song begins to play, it is "Sleigh Ride." Tonya gets three points. They guess again. (Bill goes with "The Christmas Song," and Tonya chooses "I Saw Mommy Kissing Santa Claus.")

Preparation

- Schedule a night when your group can go caroling. Be sure to choose a night when the people you will visit are likely to be home.

- Compile a list of homes to visit, along with directions.

- Decide what songs you will sing and who will lead the singing.

- Review 1 Thessalonians 5:11-12.

⚙ The next song played happens to be "Joy to the World," Bill's previous guess. That means Bill now gets one point. The score is currently Tonya: 3 and Bill: 1. On to the next guess.

AT THE SITE

1. When you arrive at the first house, tell the youth that they will be caroling. Explain that they will, however, do more than simply sing songs. The Holy Spirit will work through them to bring joy to others. Read aloud 1 Thessalonians 5:11-12. Explain that "building each other up" is a gift of the Spirit and is similar to encouragement. Tell the group that the pre-Christmas season can sometimes be very depressing and stressful for people. But God has called your group to help point others to the joy of Jesus' birth that is celebrated during this time of the year. As they sing, they will be giving others a gift from God.

2. Lead in an opening prayer and then divide the large group into small groups, if necessary, to visit and sing at the different houses and neighborhoods. Suggest that each small group choose one person to begin the singing and one person to knock on the door. Allow a minute or two for groups to decide on a beginning song and three or four additional carols. Each group should sing only the first verse of each carol. If there are children in the home, groups should sing one or two carols that children will especially enjoy. Also, tell groups to stand close to the front door or window, but not so close that youth crowd the doorway. They should begin singing even before someone opens the door.

   As the groups begin to move, remind them to be careful of plants and outside decorations, to use the sidewalks where available, and to be polite and courteous to those they visit. If some of the youth know the people in the homes they visit, they should greet them personally. Set a time and place for youth to return.

3. When the caroling is finished and youth have returned to the designated meeting spot, thank everyone for spreading joy and lifting up people. Talk about their caroling experiences: How did they feel the Holy Spirit working through them? Did they also receive joy and encouragement through the singing? How? What was a favorite experience from each small group?

4. Read aloud again 1 Thessalonians 5:11-12. Talk with the youth about why some people may be depressed during the Christmas season. Help the youth understand that often the Christmas holidays cause us to think of people and relationships we miss. Families may try to gather together, but sometimes they can't for various reasons; perhaps it's too far to travel, finances won't allow it, or it may be emotionally unhealthy for them. This is a great season for the body of Christ (the church) to be open to God's leading and to build up one another.

Bright Ideas

⚙ Recruit some church members to prepare a plate of cookies or fudge for each household you visit. Some families feel obliged to give a gift when carolers arrive; this will turn the tables, showing them that your group is all about giving love and joy.

Destination Unknown Missions 30 Excursions to Transform Your Community

Ask the following:

⚙ What other ways can God use you to encourage and bring joy to people during the holiday season?
⚙ How can you make yourself more available to God for that purpose?

5. Lead a closing prayer, asking God to bless those homes where youth sang. If possible, share some hot chocolate and Christmas cookies back at the church or someone's home.

Notes

Help your youth point others to the joy of Jesus' birth that is celebrated during the Christmas season. As they sing, they will be giving others a gift from God.

CITY STREETS

FOCUS

Youth will prepare and deliver hot soup and blankets to the homeless of a nearby city, experiencing what it means to serve "the least of these."

SCRIPTURE

Luke 14:13-14; Isaiah 58:6-7

LOCATION

A kitchen and a street in a nearby city where homeless persons gather

ABOUT THE DESTINATION

First, determine where you can take the youth to serve the homeless on a city street. Contact ministries and agencies that work in the inner city and ask if they have any suggestions for locations. Make sure they know that you plan to hand out food, as it will help them suggest a safe and appropriate location. Also ask how many homeless people live in your area. This will be helpful information for you to tell the youth.

Contact the local police department of the city you will visit and talk about the possible locations and whether there's anything you need to do or keep in mind for legal or safety reasons. Also ask if there are police units who regularly keep an eye on any of the locations.

Prior to the date of the youth visit, drive to that location at the time and on the day of the week that you plan on taking your youth. This will give you an idea of the location and surrounding area, the traffic flow, and how many people you will need to prepare to serve.

Once you have settled on a location and date and time, you will need to purchase the food and organize other donations and supplies. Soup is warm, comforting, and easy, but a wrapped sandwich that can be kept for later will be appreciated also. Announce in your church bulletin, in adult small groups, and/or Sunday school classes that you need food donations and blankets.

Preparation

- ⚙ Locate a place and set a time for serving meals to homeless persons in a nearby city.

- ⚙ Decide on the meals you will serve and grocery shop for food and supplies. Find a kitchen where you can prepare the food.

- ⚙ Provide note cards and pens for youth to write notes to the people they serve. Give the youth some suggestions about what to write.

- ⚙ Announce supply needs to your church congregation.

- ⚙ Review Luke 14:13-14 and Isaiah 58:6-7.

Ahead of time purchase or make (on a computer) note cards so that youth can write encouraging notes to accompany each meal and blanket they hand out. Also think about some ideas for youth to use in writing the notes.

Finally, work out a plan for distributing the food and blankets and be ready to communicate this plan to youth as you travel to the destination.

ON THE WAY

As the youth travel to the place where you will prepare the food (the first destination), ask them to think of all the things they do in their home: eat, sleep, play games, watch television, do homework, and so on. Make a list of every activity or task they mention. Then ask youth to consider if a home is necessary for these things to occur. Is there anything on the list that *must* take place in one's own home? Then ask:

✪ Talk with the youth about making this ministry a regular monthly trip. Depending on the travel distance, youth and adults from your church can meet after a Sunday service, prepare the food, write the notes, and travel to the city where they can hand out the food and still return before nightfall. As youth participate regularly, they will begin to look for particular people they serve each time.

✪ Since most of these activities can be accomplished anywhere, what is it that makes a home important?
✪ Why do people need a home?

AT THE SITE

1. Begin by talking about the importance of having a home. In a home you have comfort; you make and recall memories; you feel safe; and you have a place to keep your possessions. Explain to the youth that, at this destination, you will be serving the homeless. Then read aloud the two Scriptures.

2. Move to the kitchen and begin preparing the meals. Tell the youth how many people they will serve and how they will deliver the food. Assign various tasks to each youth for food preparation. This may be a learning time for some youth, as they perhaps create a meal for the first time.

   Also ask a few youth to write notes on the cards to pin to blankets or to put with the soup and sandwiches (or whatever meal you prepare). Some ideas for the notes are: "*We hope this (food or blanket) will warm you and remind you that the warmth of God's love is with you always,*" or "*May this (food or blanket) give you comfort even in the most difficult of times.*"

3. When the meal is ready, pack up the food and blankets and head for the city streets (the second destination). Along the way ask the youth what they expect to happen when they arrive. Do they know anyone who has worked with people who are homeless? Have they ever passed by homeless people on the streets? Do they ever remember people making belittling comments about the homeless (calling them names or making fun of them)? Ask, "Why do you suppose we make fun of people who are experiencing such hardship?" Remind the youth that God's Word consistently instructs us to show compassion to those who are most vulnerable. When you are nearing

your destination, be sure to go over your plan for distributing the food and blankets so that youth feel comfortable and safe with their tasks.

4. When you arrive, instruct the youth to stay together as a group. Also remind them that all of you are representatives of God's love and that your actions may be the only good news or act of kindness these people receive this day or this week.

5. When all the food and blankets have been handed out and good-byes have been said, gather the youth back into the vehicles and head back to your church or another location where you can talk together about the experience.

6. Ask for volunteers to read aloud Luke 14:13-14 and Isaiah 58:6-7. Then talk about the following:

  ❂ Why is God so concerned about people who have nothing?
  ❂ If God is concerned for them, why do they have so little?
  ❂ Why should we be concerned for those who have very little?
  ❂ Why is it difficult for people to help those who are homeless and vulnerable?

7. Close with a prayer, asking God to bless the people who received the food and blankets. Also ask youth to lift up in prayer someone they met today.

God's Word consistently instructs us to show compassion to those who are most vulnerable.

Notes

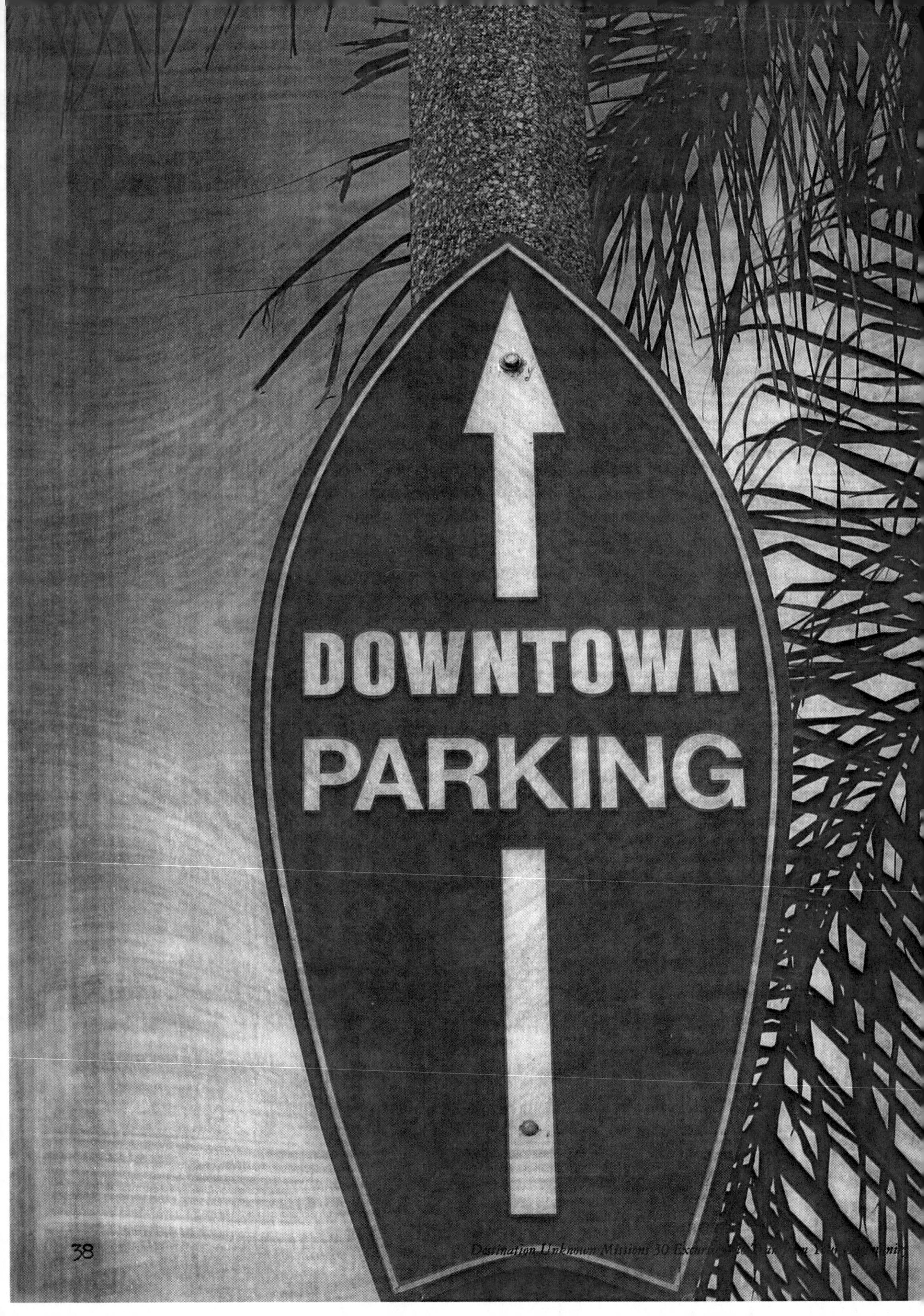
DOWNTOWN
PARKING

COMMUNITY GARDEN

FOCUS

Youth will weed and harvest at a community garden and then deliver the food to a local food bank.

SCRIPTURE

Leviticus 19:9-10

LOCATION

A nearby community garden or a vegetable garden owned by someone who will allow your group to harvest produce and then donate the food to an area food bank

ABOUT THE DESTINATION

Community gardens are popping up everywhere, and there may be more than one in your area. If not, either ask someone who is growing a private garden if you can bring your group for some light gleaning, or take a much bolder step and start a community garden through your church.

If you do plan on visiting a local community garden, do some research first. Search the Internet and find out what you can about community gardens, both in general and about your local gardens. Contact those in charge of the garden you wish to visit and set a date and time for you to bring your group.

Be sure to tell your youth to bring work gloves and to dress appropriately, wearing shoes and clothing they can get dirty.

After your group has harvested their bounty, you will need a place to deliever the food for distribution to those in need. Research local food banks in your area and make arrangements for your youth to deliver their vegetables. If possible, also arrange for your group to spend some time volunteering at the food bank, sorting donations and stocking shelves.

Preparation

✪ Identify a local community garden or contact a nearby farmer who is willing to donate some produce to an area food bank.

✪ Make sure every youth has a pair of work gloves.

✪ Contact a food bank. Arrange for a time to drop off your produce and for the youth to participate in sorting food and learning about the food bank's work.

✪ Review Leviticus 19:9-10.

ON THE WAY

As you travel to the destination, talk to the group about gardening. Ask:

- ✪ Have you ever planted or worked in a garden?
- ✪ What did you plant?
- ✪ What kind of work did you do?
- ✪ What, do you think, would life be like if you had to depend on a garden for all of the vegetables you ate?

AT THE SITE

1. Tell the youth that, throughout Scripture, God tells God's people to take care of the poor—to help them in their need and to remember that God loves them just as God loves all people. Then read aloud Leviticus 19:9-10. Explain that you and the group will pick produce in a field or garden and then take the food to a local food bank for distribution to those who most need it.

2. Spend considerable time in the garden with your group. Make sure you are not only picking but also tending to the garden. Pulling weeds and watering (if needed) will help the garden thrive, which will then also help those who rely on the food.

3. When you have picked the food you need and have spent some time caring for the garden, place all the produce in one spot. Ask the group to join hands around the food gathered and say a blessing, thanking God for the way we are allowed to share in God's love for all people. Pray also for those who will receive the food, asking that they recognize that it is God who has supplied the food for them.

4. Deliever the food to the food bank and spend some time there helping. Find out all you can about how the food bank works. Encourage the youth to ask questions at the food bank, such as:

- ✪ How does the food bank distribute food to people in the community who need it?
- ✪ How did the food bank get started, and how long has it been serving the community?
- ✪ What are some of the biggest challenges that come with running a food bank?
- ✪ During what times of year are needs the greatest?

5. Before you depart, talk with the group about how they might continue to help the poor in their community. Read aloud again Leviticus 19:9-10. Ask: "We know that the Bible tells us that God loves all people, but why does God so often focus on the poor and hungry? Why do we need to be

Bright Ideas

- ✪ Talk with the youth and some avid gardeners in your church about starting a community garden through your congregation. You can start small for the first few years and then expand as interest increases. You can either donate the food to agencies for distribution or make it available to anyone who would like to come and work the garden.

- ✪ Consider this destination in conjunction with the "A Neighborhood and Food Pantry" (see page 55), making one full day of gathering food from neighbors and fields.

- ✪ Consider contacting area farmers to schedule a day of gleaning (picking up any produce left after harvesting). Rather than being wasted, the gleaned food can help feed those who depend your local food bank or shelter.

reminded of the poor and their needs? A farmer who left food at the edges of his field for the poor was always reminded of the needs of the poor (and God's love for them), even while he had so much food. When we have abundance, or don't have to worry about meeting basic needs, we also need to find ways to remind ourselves of the poor and of God's commands to love and serve them."

6. Thank the people at the food bank and the youth who worked today, then return to your church.

God tells God's people to take care of the poor—
to help them in their need and to remember that God
loves them just as God loves all people.

Notes

COMMUNITY LUNCH

FOCUS

Youth will visit a local agency that provides meals to persons in need, showing Christ's love by eating and visiting with the other guests and welcoming them into youth's lives. Youth will also follow Christ's example of service by helping with cleanup afterward.

SCRIPTURES

Luke 14:16-24

LOCATION

A local agency or ministry that provides meals to persons in need

Preparation

⚙ Contact an agency or group in your community that provides meals to people who are homeless and/or hungry. Explain that your group would like to eat a meal as guests. Offer to help with cleanup.

⚙ Review Luke 14:16-24.

ABOUT THE DESTINATION

Many communities have an agency or group that provides meals to persons and families who are homeless or lack enough money for food. Contact one of these providers and, instead of volunteering your group to prepare or serve a meal (which is also a great outreach for your youth to experience), explain that you would like to bring some youth to eat and visit with the other guests. Too often when we reach out to those in need, we build barriers by only serving them physically and not taking the time to get to know them. What would happen if you and your youth were to actually befriend some of the needy people in your community? Would you find ways to serve them throughout the year instead of only eating a meal with them?

As you talk with the agency to schedule a date and time, tell them you would like to help with cleanup afterward as a way to pay for your group's food. Also ask if there are any regular guests who could use some company or extra help at home and consider ways to help meet those needs in the days ahead.

When Jesus said, "I was a stranger and you welcomed me" (Matthew 25:35c), he wasn't talking just about helping the stranger feel welcome in our church buildings (which certainly is something that needs improvement in most churches). He was also referring to how we welcome people into our lives—into our group of friends and into our community. Your youth can learn a lot about

the needy in your community—their struggles, their joys, their stories, and even things they have in common—by getting to know them within the safety of a community meal program.

On the Way

If possible, travel as a group to your location and talk about what it must be like to have to rely upon others' giving. Would that make you more humble or more cynical? How do you think you would feel on days when help isn't available? How would it affect your understanding of God's grace?

At the Site

1. Gather first in a location apart from the other guests (perhaps a meeting room or even the van or bus you rode while traveling to the location). Reveal to the youth why you are at this site. Explain that, although volunteering to serve is important, that is not why you are here today. Emphasize that you are here to get to know the people who come here to eat. Tell the youth they will eat with the guests, getting to know them and helping them feel welcome and comfortable. Remind the youth that, in many ways, they will be the "outsiders" in the dining room today.

2. Invite a volunteer to read aloud the parable of the banquet from Luke 14:16-24. Ask:

   ❂ How does this Scripture apply to what we are doing here today?
   ❂ What does it say about the people with whom we should spend time and have meals?

   Point out that, after the host asks his servant to invite "the poor, crippled, blind, and lame" (verse 21), he asks the servant also to invite anyone and everyone who is willing to come. The parable is not just about dining with persons who are outsiders or in need; it is about removing all the barriers that keep us from sharing food and fellowship with our neighbors.

3. Give the youth ideas for topics to talk about while dining with the other guests. Also suggest ideas for gathering information about the guests they meet. Remind the youth to listen closely to what people say and to ask questions that build on these conversations. For example, if a person says that he or she has been eating there for a long time, a youth might respond, "You must either like the food or the company to come here so often." If a guest asks a youth why he or she is there, the youth might answer, "We realized that we are missing out on getting to know some of our neighbors, and we wanted to share a meal with you." Encourage the youth not to dominate a conversation and to spread out among the guests.

Bright Ideas

❂ Contact some of your local elected officials (the mayor, a city council member, the county commissioner, and so on) and/or your senior pastor and invite them to join you and your group on this outing. It would be good for public servants to also meet and get to know the stories of the less fortunate in your area.

4. Join the other guests in the dining room. Try to be in the dining room before the prayer, if one is offered. Quietly remind youth to spread out as they sit down to eat.

5. When the meal is over, thank the guests for allowing youth to visit and eat with them. Also thank the volunteers who prepared and served the meal. Then help clean up and prepare the room for the next gathering.

6. Find a place where you and your group can talk about the lunch experience. Meet in the dining hall (after it has been cleaned and set up), a nearby room, or back at your church. Talk about what happened: What made conversation easy? What made it difficult? What did you learn from the people you met? What life lessons did you learn today?

7. Read aloud again the parable from Luke. Ask the youth if this Bible passage has new meaning to them after this experience. Talk about other ways they can break down barriers that separate them from their neighbors. How might what they learned today also apply to their lunchroom at school?

8. Close in prayer. During the prayer allow each person in the group to offer a name and/or a short prayer for someone he or she met during the meal.

Notes

Door to Door

Focus

Youth will go door to door in a local neighborhood, collecting supplies for use in disaster relief emergency health kits, then assemble the kits for shipping and delivery as needed.

Scriptures

Isaiah 61:1-6

Location

A safe neighborhood in which youth can walk door to door to collect supplies

About the Destination

There is always some sort of large-scale disaster in the world that needs our attention. The problem is that our attention quickly moves on to the next big breaking news story, and we often forget the places that still need disaster relief. You and your group can help those who have experienced disaster by collecting essential items for health kits and sending those kits to assisting agencies.

Compile a list of the types of items needed for the disaster relief kits. Also include the name and contact information of your church, along with an explanation of where the donated supplies will be sent. If you have a computer, type up the list of needed supplies and print enough copies for youth to leave one at each house visited so that people can donate later, if they choose.

Ahead of time, call some local drug stores to see if they can supply some of the items needed. If so, make arrangements to have these supplies picked up.

The United Methodist Committee on Relief (UMCOR) is one disaster-response organization that collects and distributes relief supplies. Check the website, *www. umcor.org*, for specific instructions about assembling kits, up-to-date information on the parts of the world that are in need of relief, and how to transport relief supplies to the people who need them.

Preparation

⚙ Decide on a neighborhood for door-to-door collections.

⚙ Print copies of supplies needed (one per house visited), along with contact information for your church and an explanation of where the donations will be sent.

⚙ Research instructions for assembling kits and make available while doing so.

⚙ Check to see if your state has any restrictions on door-to-door solicitation so that you don't inadvertently break any laws.

⚙ Review Isaiah 61:1-6.

ADVENTURE

On the Way

While driving to the neighborhood, ask the youth what they know about places that have experienced disasters in recent years. Ask:

- Do you remember seeing pictures or video of the devastation?
- What would you do if such a disaster struck our community? (Or, what did you do when such a disaster struck our community?)
- Whom would you (or did you) turn to for help in such a situation?
- When have you had to depend on help from a stranger? What was that like?

At the Site

1. Explain that youth will be going out in teams of two or three to ask for donations for emergency health kits distributed for disaster relief. Hand out the printed lists for youth to leave with each donor. Remind the youth to be especially courteous when making their requests and to refrain from judging if a person cannot give at this time.

2. Read aloud Isaiah 61:1-6. Explain to the youth that they, like Isaiah, are sent out to bring relief to the afflicted and to help "renew ruined cities" (verse 4). Lead in a short prayer, asking God to help youth be mindful of their calling as they collect supplies.

3. Send out the teams, telling them how much time they have to collect and where you will meet them at the end of that time.

4. When you meet the youth at the end of the collection time, return to the church or to a central meeting place to assemble the emergency kits. Be prepared to purchase a few more supplies to even out all that was collected and complete each kit. Make sure instructions for how to arrange the kits are available as youth work.

5. When all the kits are assembled, take a picture of the group and the kits. Post the picture on a church bulletin board and/or on the church website.

6. Close this gathering with a prayer for God to bless the kits and to bring a feeling of peace and security to those who are going through such hardships. Thank God for calling your youth to bring relief to others.

Bright Ideas

- If someone in your congregation has served on a recent mission trip to a disaster location, invite that person to speak with your youth before they go out seeking donations. This will add a more personal aspect to their ministry.

ELEMENTARY SCHOOL

FOCUS

Youth will tutor students at an elementary school, building relationships with younger children. They also will spend time considering those adults who have been influential in their individual lives.

SCRIPTURE

1 Timothy 1:1-4

LOCATION

A classroom or school setting where you can oversee youth as they work individually helping younger students with their homework

ABOUT THE DESTINATION

Research the area to find a local school that already has an afterschool tutoring program in place and schedule a time when you can bring your group to help. Ask what kind of requirements should be met before your group visits (such as background checks or signed permission slips). Also ask if there are any young children with particular needs and attempt to match those needs with some of your youth who are especially gifted in those areas. For example, if a child needs special help with math, recruit a youth who is a whiz with numbers. Also recruit some youth who are particularly good and experienced at working with children. They can serve as examples for other youth who might not have much experience.

Toward the end of the debriefing time (see page 51), youth will be encouraged to think of someone with whom they might develop a faith-mentoring relationship. These should be strong, devoted Christians who would take the responsibility seriously. The youth will not be looking for "friends" to fill this role, but for strong believers who can strengthen and support them on their faith journeys. Be prepared for a few youth to name you or a member of the church's pastoral staff as their choice for this faith mentor. While this is an honor, it may also be a perceived "expected" response. Remember, a pastor or youth leader may have many relationships like this, making it difficult to offer the individual time that some youth need. Consider "mentoring" that youth into a faith relationship with another church member in addition to yourself or a pastor.

Preparation

❂ Check with the school about necessary requirements, releases, or permission slips and make sure those are complete prior to the destination date.

❂ Ask the school about any children with particular needs.

❂ Compile a list of possible church members to serve as mentors to youth.

❂ Review 1 Timothy 1:1-4.

Plan to arrive at the destination at least fifteen minutes before the children arrive so that you can read aloud the Scripture and spend some time talking about expectations for the tutoring time. Alert youth that you will meet for about thirty minutes after the tutoring session to debrief.

On the Way

Point out that children tend to look up to older youth, especially when respect and trust are present. Ask the youth to name some people in their lives (other than parents) who have affected or influenced them in positive ways. Ask the youth to talk about how these persons have had an impact on their lives? How did they know they could trust them? What have the youth learned from these adults that they can apply to their relationships with younger children?

At the Site

1. Begin with a short explanation of what youth will be doing. Encourage the youth to tell the students a little about themselves in order to help the younger students feel more comfortable. Remind them to thank the children at the end of the tutoring session for allowing them to help.

2. Read aloud 1 Timothy 1:1-4. Explain that Timothy, the person to whom Paul was writing, was a young man whom Paul had helped to bring up in Christian faith. Scripture tells us that Timothy traveled extensively with Paul, visited Paul in prison, was a prisoner himself at times because of his faith and teachings, and served as a leader in the church of Ephesus, which Paul and Timothy had helped start. Paul called Timothy his "child in the faith," describing the mentor-type bond he shared with him. Explain that the youth will begin a teaching-and-helping relationship with the young students they help today.

3. After giving background information on Paul and Timothy's relationship, read aloud the Scripture again. Lead the youth in a short prayer, asking that they be receptive to how God will use them during their time with the children.

4. When the children arrive, introduce the youth to the students they will be tutoring. As they work with the young students, move around the room and listen to conversations and interactions. Be careful not to step in too quickly if you think a youth is having trouble. The relationship is built and strengthened by experiencing differences and recognizing ways to adapt to those differences. Your most important role as leader in this scenario is communicating that you are available for support but not necessarily to bail youth out of a tough or challenging situation. When the tutoring time is nearly over, give the youth some sort of signal to finish up and thank the children for allowing them to help.

Bright Ideas

◉ When this activity is over, ask those who participated to consider volunteering to tutor through this program on a monthly or weekly basis. The relationships they have established can become something powerful and nurturing to the younger children, influencing them for years to come.

5. After the children are gone, meet with the youth either in the same room or another nearby location. Discuss what happened during their session. Ask: "On a scale of 1 to 10 (10 being the best), how well do you think you connected to the child you tutored? What helped or hindered your relationship today? What might have helped more? How did the child you worked with remind you of yourself at that age? How might you be able to help this child in the future? How might God use what you did today to help this student grow in faith?"

6. Now ask the youth to recall the people they mentioned earlier who have been influential and helpful in their lives. Ask:

- ⦿ Who has had the strongest impact (in a positive way) on your faith life so far? How or why?
- ⦿ Is it possible for you to develop or continue the relationship with that person? If not, is there someone else who could mentor you in your faith life? Why would this be helpful?
- ⦿ How might God work through your relationship with a mentor?

Encourage youth to talk to some of the people they mentioned to see if they are interested in being their faith mentors. If there are some youth who are new to your group and don't know many adults in your church yet, tell them you have a list of names of potential mentors. Offer to introduce the youth to these adults. Follow up with youth in the days ahead.

7. Gather the youth in a circle and lead a closing prayer. Explain that you will open the prayer and then each youth should name aloud the child he or she tutored and offer up words of thanks and care for that student. Close the prayer by asking God to guide your youth in their relationships so that they not only will influence others but also will find strong, faithful Christian mentors who will give them support and insight.

Notes

FIRE HYDRANTS

FOCUS

Youth will paint city fire hydrants and discuss the importance of serving their community.

SCRIPTURE

Nehemiah 2:17-18

LOCATION

Along the streets in your community

ABOUT THE DESTINATION

Contact the public utilities or public works department of your city and inquire about repainting fire hydrants. If they have work for you to do and are willing to supply the paint—then this is a great service opportunity for your youth.

Ahead of time gather or purchase enough paintbrushes for all the youth who will participate in this project. Also tell your youth to dress in clothing that they don't mind getting stained or messy.

ON THE WAY

Ask the youth to think about areas of their community that need improvement. Focus on public places—places owned by the county or city and open to everyone—rather than on privately owned property. Talk about the effects that such places have on the people who live around them. How does it affect the mood of people in the community when these public places are well kept? How does it affect their mood when these places are not maintained properly?

Preparation

✪ Contact your local public utilities or public works department and ask about repainting fire hydrants. Also ask if they will supply the paint.

✪ Gather or purchase paintbrushes for all youth who will work on this project.

✪ Enlist two adult volunteers for every four or five youth.

✪ Review Nehemiah 2:17-18.

Bright Ideas

⚙ Contact local news media and inform them of ways your youth are stepping up to help the community.

AT THE SITE

1. When you arrive at the first hydrant you will paint, gather everyone around the hydrant and provide some background information about Nehemiah. Explain that Nehemiah was in charge of rebuilding the wall of Jerusalem several decades after the Babylonians had destroyed the city. Nehemiah returned to Jerusalem to find the city in ruins and the people devastated by the destruction that surrounded them. The state of the once great city left the people feeling hopeless. Nehemiah believed that bringing the people together on an important, measurable task would unite them behind a cause, raise their hopes and confidence, and bring new life to their beloved city. So Nehemiah organized the people to rebuild the wall surrounding Jerusalem. Every family in Judah except one helped rebuild the wall.

2. Read aloud Nehemiah 2:17-18. Tell the youth that they will be painting fire hydrants—a seemingly simple and trivial task, but one that will save the city money and will help beautify the community. Give the youth any instructions they need to complete the project and hand out the paintbrushes. Explain that the city provided the paint, so they shouldn't waste it.

3. Drop off teams of four or five youth (each with two unrelated adults for safety and supervision) at each fire hydrant. Make sure the teams know where to go when they finish a hydrant. If each team is painting multiple hydrants, make sure they know where all their assigned hydrants are located and how to get to them.

4. When the youth have finished their painting, meet together at an ice-cream shop or someplace for a light snack and talk about the service they provided for their community. Remind the youth of the Scripture from Nehemiah. Ask:

    ⚙ How did people respond today when they saw what you were doing?
    ⚙ How does volunteering in your community affect the people of the community?
    ⚙ What kinds of other volunteer opportunities are you aware of in our community? Which of these service opportunities are appealing to you?

5. Close with a prayer for your city, asking God to motivate more and more people to care for their public areas.

A Food Pantry and a Neighborhood

Focus

Youth will gather food items during a neighborhood "scavenger hunt," learn about hunger and food insecurity in their area, and then deliver the food items to a local food pantry that serves the needs of the community. At the pantry youth will learn about how it serves others and how to volunteer to help in its ministry.

Scripture

Isaiah 58:10

Location

A neighborhood where some of your youth live and a food pantry in your community

About the Destination

This service opportunity includes two destinations. The first one is a local neighborhood. Choose a safe, residential area where youth can walk from house to house, asking for donations to a local food pantry. A week or so ahead of time, post a few signs around the neighborhood alerting residents that youth will be going door to door collecting food donations. (If possible, and if an e-mail list is available, notify residents using this method.)

The second destination is the food pantry where you will deliver the food you collect. Many communities have some sort of center where people can go to receive basic food in cases of emergency. Check with other local churches or social service agencies for locations near you. Call the pantry you choose and ask about specific needs for the season. They may have plenty of cereal items but need canned food, or they may need particular kinds of canned food. Explain that you will be collecting food and would like to bring your group by to deliver what is collected as well as learn about the work of the food pantry. Ask if someone would be available to lead a tour and explain to youth how a person can volunteer in the future.

Also ask for any available fliers or brochures that youth could leave at the homes where they ask for food donations, along with any statistics about homelessness or poverty in the area. Check the United States Census Bureau website at *www.census. gov* for additional information.

ON THE WAY

While driving to the neighborhood for the scavenger hunt, talk with the youth about their willingness (or nonwillingness) to ask someone for help. How bad does a situation have to get before they reach out for help? Why are we sometimes afraid to ask for help? How willing are they to help someone else? What determines if they will help someone or not? How do they respond if a stranger asks for help?

AT THE SITE

1. Tell the youth that they are going on two trips today. First, they will go door to door in a neighborhood, asking people to donate food for the local food pantry. Then, after collecting the food, they will deliver it to the local food bank.

2. Tell the group some of the statistical information you learned about hunger and poverty in your area (which you researched ahead of time). This information is important, because it can help the youth understand that the scavenger hunt is more than a game. Emphasize that they are about to embark on an act of justice, bringing food to the hungry and hope to those in despair. Next, read aloud Isaiah 58 and explain that God is speaking to a people who enjoy worship and prayer but who also wonder why it seems that God is not listening to them. God answers this question through the prophet, telling them that their worship and prayers are selfish—offered for their personal enjoyment and their individual gain. God tells God's people that they must seek justice in their land by looking out for the needs of the poor and hungry. After the Scripture reading, ask the youth what kind of response they think God and the prophet want or expect from these words.

3. Divide the group into teams of three or four, and assign two adults to each group. Explain that this is a food scavenger hunt and that each team will try to earn points by collecting the various kinds of food on a list. Hand out a few empty grocery bags to each group and a copy of the points list (or one like it) on the following page. Remind the youth to be courteous while collecting the food.

4. When everyone has returned, tally the points and award the team that collected the most points the title of "Über Food Gatherer." Then load the food into a vehicle and take the food and the youth to deliver the bounty to the food pantry.

5. On the way to the food pantry, ask at least three different people, one at a time, to read aloud Isaiah 58:10.

6. At the food pantry, ask the youth to carry in their donations. If you have time, and if the food pantry allows you to do so, help shelve or box the

Preparation

✪ Verify if your state has any restrictions on door-to-door solicitation so that you don't inadvertently break any laws

Bright Ideas

✪ If you have time, offer to help sort food at the food pantry when you deliver what you collected. (You may have to schedule a return trip.) Doing this will help the youth feel more comfortable about volunteering in the future and also will help them better understand how the pantry serves the community.

✪ If you have trouble scheduling both of these destinations in one day, try switching the order and visiting the pantry first; then do the scavenger hunt after dinner when the pantry might be closed. Another option would be to visit each destination on a different day.

various kinds of food in the appropriate places. If possible, take a tour of the food pantry. Encourage your youth to ask questions about the people the pantry serves, how many people are served each day, how often the stock is depleted, and how a person can volunteer to serve. If possible, ask for business cards or fliers about the pantry and give one to each participant who is interested in volunteering.

7. Conclude your time at the pantry with a prayer for the people who are served through its work and for the volunteers who work at the pantry. Ask God to bless the food your youth donated today and the people who receive it.

Bright Ideas

Food Scavenger Hunt

Use this list to tally the points for your team as you collect food donations. An item of food can earn multiple points. Remember to be courteous at each home, since you are representing not only yourself and your family but also the church and the food pantry we are helping. You have one hour to collect your food and return.

_____	Every food item	5 points
_____	Any type of green vegetable	50 points
_____	Any kind of canned meat	50 points
_____	Chili	30 points
_____	A can with a pull-top lid	30 points
_____	Pudding	20 points
_____	Breakfast cereal	20 points
_____	Weighs more than one pound	30 points
_____	Contains rice	20 points
_____	Pasta	15 points

TOTAL _____

⦿ If you cannot find a nearby food pantry, then your task just became more involved and more exciting. God may be calling you and your youth to help start one in your community. Plan to visit a food pantry in a nearby city and take along some youth and leaders from your church. Take extensive notes.

FREE LUNCHES

FOCUS

Youth will hand out free lunches at a busy intersection, demonstrating God's grace to people of the community, and discuss the ways people respond to such free gifts.

SCRIPTURE

John 6:33-35; Romans 8:35-39

LOCATION

An intersection with a traffic light (or an all-way stop) and an available corner where your group can set up a drive-by lunch stand and hand out free lunches to those waiting at the stop light

ABOUT THE DESTINATION

It is always interesting how people respond to God's grace. We live in a society that says, "There is no such thing as a free lunch." Well, this destination will prove society wrong. It is important for people to understand that God's blessing of salvation is free. While handing out free lunches is not the same as God's powerful grace, it is an attention-grabber and shows people that your church is willing to communicate God's unconditional love to anyone who will accept it.

Choose an intersection with a traffic light and at least one corner (a vacant lot works best) where you can set up a table, a cooler stocked with packed lunches, and a sign that reads, "Wave for a Free Lunch . . . Really!" Ahead of time check with the landowner of the corner for permission to set up. Also research any state or local laws that would prohibit you from moving forward with the activity.

If this destination is truly a surprise for the youth, then either ask a few people from the church to help you prepare the lunches a day ahead or ask the youth to meet and prepare the lunches without telling them why. Make sure to provide a lunch that will not spoil quickly. Contents might include a sandwich, a small package of individually wrapped crackers, an apple or other piece of fruit, a juice box or similar drink, and perhaps a cookie or other small, individually wrapped dessert. Also include in the bag a copy of the following statement (or a similar one; see page 127):

Preparation

- ⊙ Research state or local laws related to this activity.

- ⊙ Check with the landowner for permission to set up on the corner you choose.

- ⊙ Prepare lunches and pack in coolers.

- ⊙ Make copies of the statement on page 60 to include in lunch bags.

- ⊙ Prepare a sign that says: "Wave for a Free Lunch . . . Really!"

- ⊙ Review John 6:33-35; Romans 8:35-39.

Thank you for accepting this free lunch. We hope it will remind you that God's love is free to you at all times. In fact, there is nothing you can do that will take away God's love. Read Romans 8:35-39. Have a great day!

—Your free lunch crew at {add church name, address, and phone number}

ON THE WAY

As you drive to the corner of the intersection, ask the youth if they have ever heard the saying, "There's no such thing as a free lunch." Talk about what they think the statement means. Is the statement true? Why or why not? Can you think of anything that is totally free?

AT THE SITE

1. Gather youth around you as you read aloud John 6:33-35. Ask: "What is the bread that Jesus mentions? How does such bread take away hunger? What kind of hunger is Jesus talking about?"

2. Ask the youth to notice the people driving by as you explain that many of these passers-by are hungering for something more. They try to fill their lives with material things or with relationships. Yet they continue to hunger for something more. Jesus teaches that we hunger for God's love. Ask, "What can we do right now that will help these people know a little more about God's love?"

3. Tell the youth that the prepared sack lunches are for the people driving past. Ask the youth to set up the table and the sign. Tell them to take one or two lunch bags each, stand on the corner, and hand a free lunch to anyone who waves. Explain that they should not accept donations. If anyone offers a donation, the youth should explain that the lunches are truly free—no strings attached. If a person insists on giving a donation, youth should say that the church address is inside the bag if they would like to contact someone. The youth may also suggest that, in lieu of a donation, the person can "pay it forward" by doing something nice and "free" for someone else. Ask the youth to pay attention to the ways that people respond to the free lunch.

4. After all the lunches have been given away, gather the youth together and talk about what they experienced. Ask:

   ✪ How did people respond?
   ✪ Who was the most gracious person you encountered?
   ✪ Did anyone ignore us completely? Why, do you think, did they ignore us?
   ✪ Why, do you think, did some people accept the gift?
   ✪ What did you do that made people more willing to take a lunch?

✸ What kinds of things does the church do that helps people be open to learning about God's love?

✸ What kinds of things does the church do that makes people want to ignore the church?

5. Close with a prayer, asking God to bless those who gained a better understanding of God's love today. Also ask God to help the Christian community be more understanding of what people hunger for and how we, the church, can help people satisfy that hunger.

Notes

Is it true that there's no such thing as a free lunch?

Funeral Meal

Focus

Youth will plan and serve a meal for people who have just attended a funeral, serving others through care and comfort during a time of sadness.

Scripture

2 Corinthians 1:3-5

Location

A funeral home

About the Destination

This destination will take some time to organize and plan, but the help and comfort it provides will be worth the effort.

A common tradition following a funeral is the gathering of family and friends to enjoy a meal together, while sharing stories and fond memories of the deceased. Often the planning of such a meal falls on the shoulders of the deceased's family members, adding more stress at a time when life is already difficult. A pre-planned and prepared meal is extremely helpful to a family who has recently suffered loss.

First, contact a funeral home director and schedule a time when you and your group can visit and talk about ways to care for those who mourn the loss of a loved one. Ask if the funeral home director can offer a short tour and spend some time answering any questions youth may have. If the director is unavailable, ask the pastor of your church to accompany your group to the funeral home and talk with the youth.

During the discussion at the funeral home, present the idea of planning and providing a funeral meal. If the group decides that they would like to carry out this activity in the weeks ahead, notify the funeral home director and/or the pastor of your church, explaining that you and your group would like to provide a funeral meal if or when the need arises.

Preparation

✪ Contact a local funeral home and schedule a visit.

✪ Decide on the location for preparing food and hosting the meal.

✪ Plan the menu, discuss logistics, and decide on necessary supplies.

✪ Compile a list of church members to contact about preparing food.

✪ Distribute appropriate contact information.

✪ Review 2 Corinthians 1:3-5.

Bright Ideas

☘ Consider starting this after-funeral meal as an ongoing ministry offered by your church. The ministry should include those who will serve, those who will contact people when needed, and those who will cook and prepare food.

Also, decide on a location to host the meal. A full kitchen is not necessary, since people can prepare the dishes in their homes ahead of time and deliver the food before the guests arrive. A fellowship hall at the church may be the ideal space for such a gathering.

On the Way

As you travel to the funeral home, ask the youth if they have ever attended a funeral. For whom? Who attended? What happened during the funeral? What happened after the funeral? If none have experienced a funeral, ask them to tell what they think may happen during this time.

Remind youth to speak softly while touring the funeral home, being mindful of any families who may be present and grieving.

At the Site

1. Introduce your group to the funeral home director and allow him or her to show the group around the funeral home.

2. After the tour, move to a place where everyone in your group can sit and talk with either the funeral director or a pastor. Encourage the group to ask questions. Focus on the compassion for those who mourn by asking what kinds of services the funeral home and the pastor offer to provide comfort for those struggling with the death of a loved one.

3. Tell the group about an act of service that you would like for them to consider. Explain that, after a funeral, people often gather together for a meal and to share stories and memories of the deceased. It is one way to support one another during a time of grief. Point out how helpful it would be to provide such a meal, and ask the group if they would like to help plan a menu and enlist folks to prepare food and help serve when the need arises.

4. If the youth are willing to offer this service, plan the menu and discuss logistics. Talk about how the room should be set up: where the serving table will be located, the size of the tables where people will be seated, and the number of chairs at each table. Also plan for items such as tablecloths, dishes, napkins, and silverware. Finally, talk about the meal itself. Consider a "covered dish" or buffet style, eliminating the need for servers at every table. However, you should enlist a few servers to fill drink glasses and to check tables to see if there's anything they can do for the guests (a forgotten napkin, a glass of water, and so on).

Compile a list of names of people in the church to contact about preparing the food, and decide on the types of food you will request. Keep the menu streamlined by serving fried chicken or ham, a few salads, two vegetables, bread or rolls, dessert, and drink (water, tea, and coffee), or something equally as simple. Do your best to provide options for people who have varying dietary needs (vegetarians, people with gluten allergies, and so on).

Determine who in your group will contact the food preparers. They should explain that the group is planning for a future meal on a date yet to be determined and, at this point, asking only if they can call on them later to prepare one of the dishes and deliver it to the specified location on the day of the funeral.

5. When plans are complete, ask three different youth, one after another, to read aloud 2 Corinthians 1:3-5. Then ask the youth for their insight on the Scripture: What does the passage have to do with helping others? What do the words "consolation" or "comfort," and "afflictions" mean? What, according to Paul (who wrote 2 Corinthians as a letter to the church he had started in Corinth), is our source of help when we console others? Explain that this meal is a way that God will show consolation and comfort to people through our service.

6. Inform the pastor and funeral home director of your intentions to provide a meal. Provide your phone number so they can contact you when a family might want to request your service.

7. Close with a prayer for those you may soon be serving. Remind youth to prepare for their upcoming time of service by praying daily for the people you will serve.

8. Make sure everyone has the necessary contact information so that, when you are asked to provide a funeral meal, you can quickly notify servers, preparers, and the family in need.

Notes

Destination Unknown: Mission 30: Encounter—Transform Your Community

GROCERY STORE

FOCUS

Youth will return grocery carts and clean restrooms at a local grocery store to learn about serving without receiving recognition and how every act we do should bring glory to God and not ourselves.

SCRIPTURE

Matthew 6:1-4; 2 Corinthians 10:17

LOCATION

A local grocery store or shopping center

ABOUT THE DESTINATION

Local marketplaces are important to the community. People travel daily or weekly to purchase what they need at these places of business. Youth can serve the people of your community by performing helpful tasks behind the scenes.

Contact a local store and ask permission for your group to clean the restrooms, pick up trash in the parking lot, and return shopping carts left outside the store. These chores won't take much time, so ask a number of stores and food markets and gas stations in your area. When a business agrees, be sure to tell others you call that you already have a few commitments but that you need additional jobs. Don't be disappointed if they turn down your offer. Some people are paid for these tasks, and you don't want to take away their jobs.

Also explain to business owners that you don't want the group to be recognized for their help and that they will do the work quickly and quietly and move on. Tell them also that you will not tell the youth that you have asked permission for them to do the work, because you want them to learn the importance of doing random acts of kindness without receiving recognition. Emphasize that you are calling to receive permission so there will be no misunderstandings when youth arrive and begin quietly cleaning a restroom or a parking lot.

Without giving away your destination, tell youth to wear work clothes that may get dirty. Also provide throw-away gloves for picking up trash and cleaning restrooms.

Preparation

- ✪ Contact local grocery stores, markets, and gas stations to ask if youth can clean bathrooms, return carts, and perform other services.

- ✪ Purchase throw-away gloves for youth to wear while picking up trash and cleaning restrooms.

- ✪ Review Matthew 6:1-4 and 2 Corinthians 10:17.

ADVENTURE

ON THE WAY

Ask the youth why they like to help people. Encourage them to offer more than one answer. Some will say that they like seeing the effect it has on those who receive the help. Others may say that it is because they have been helped themselves and they want to pay it forward. Acknowledge all of their responses as viable, good reasons. Then ask:

- ☻ What would helping others be like if the recipients never knew you that you helped?
- ☻ What if you knew that you would never receive recognition for helping someone else? Would you still help?

AT THE SITE

1. When you arrive at your first business location, read aloud Jesus' teaching from Matthew 6:1-4. Ask:

- ☻ Who usually receives recognition when someone sees you doing the work?
- ☻ Who gives you credit for doing such work?
- ☻ If you do something in secret, as Jesus suggests, who sees it? Whom does Jesus say will give you recognition for those things done in secret?

2. Explain that on this day the group will serve in secret. Tell them they will complete the following tasks at this and following locations, then will move on to other businesses and do the same. As you talk about each task, hand out the throw-away gloves.

- ☻ Pick up trash in the parking lot.
- ☻ Return shopping carts. (It is OK if people see the youth doing this, but the youth shouldn't make a big deal about volunteering and shouldn't say that they are doing it as part of a church group activity.)
- ☻ Clean the store's restrooms.

3. Show the youth (by your example) how to do such work with a gracious spirit, never complaining, never seeking recognition, and always seeking ways to help. (Watch how people respond and talk about reactions in later discussion.)

4. After you have finished the work at all the scheduled destinations, find a comfortable place where you all can talk about your experiences. Read aloud again Matthew 6:1-4. Tell the group that Jesus was responding to the religious leaders who would show off their piety (their righteous acts). Ask and talk about the following:

Bright Ideas

IDEA

- ☻ Combine this activity with the "Rake and Run" destination (on page 93) for more experience in outreach without recognition.

Destination Unknown Missions 30 Excursions to Transform Your Community

⊗ Why is it dangerous to become prideful and boisterous about the good and kind acts you do?

⊗ How can you do good works without boasting about them?

⊗ What is the difference between offering all you do for God's glory and doing what God wants you to do? Can you do both?

5. Now read aloud 2 Corinthians 10:17. Say: "One way to 'boast' about good works is by boasting about what God does. 'Boasting in the Lord,' (NRSV) as Paul calls it, is proclaiming the works that God does through God's people. It brings God credit instead of keeping the recognition for ourselves."

6. Close in prayer, asking God to bless the work everyone did and allow it to bring God glory. Thank God for the lives of those who were touched by such works and ask for their continued growth in Christ.

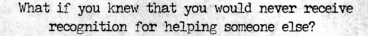

What if you knew that you would never receive recognition for helping someone else?

Notes

HIKING TRAIL

FOCUS

Youth will help to reclaim a local hiking trail and learn about its history and significance for the community. The activity will also serve as a metaphor for how God leads us on paths of truth.

SCRIPTURE

Psalm 23:3; 25:4-5

LOCATION

A local trail or path that needs to be cleared and cleaned

ABOUT THE DESTINATION

When deciding which path or trail to clear in or near your community, talk to the city or county parks department. A recent storm may have blown down trees or branches that need to be cut and cleared quickly at a popular walking or hiking trail. Also, do some research to learn about any trails around your community that have particular historical significance. An interesting story or historical connection to a trail can help make the work more interesting and more meaningful to the youth.

A few days before you bring your group to work, visit the trail and surrounding area that needs clearing. This is important because you will get an idea of the types of tools you will need and how your group can prepare for the work they will do. Take a close look at the trail and consider what and how much you and your group are capable of doing. Are benches or steps needed? Handrails? Can you provide these items? If not, ask around to see if there are people in your church community who also would want to help. Remind youth to wear appropriate work clothes and to bring work gloves.

In addition to determining the type work and tools needed, check around to see if there are nearby restroom facilities. Also, plan to take a cooler of water or water bottles. If you think it will take most of the day to accomplish the clearing and cleaning tasks, enlist some church members to provide snacks or sack lunches.

Preparation

⚙ Locate a path or trail in or near your community that needs repair or improvement.

⚙ Determine the amount of work that needs to be accomplished and gather the necessary equipment and tools.

⚙ Provide a cooler of water or water bottles and, if necessary, enlist church members to provide snacks or sack lunches.

⚙ Review Psalm 23:3; 25:4-5.

ADVENTURE

ON THE WAY

Invite the youth to think of their lives as a journey along a path. Ask:

- ☼ What does your path look like?
- ☼ What sorts of twists and turns and switchbacks have you walked through so far?
- ☼ What sorts of obstacles have you had to go over or around?
- ☼ What does the path look like where you are right now?

AT THE SITE

1. When you arrive, tell your group what you know about the trail (if there is historical significance) and explain the type of work that needs to be accomplished. Assign specific tasks. Hand out the tools and make sure people know the proper ways to use them.

2. Before youth begin, tell them that you want them to reflect on their individual life paths while working. Point out that Scripture sometimes speaks of our walk with God as if we are following God's path. Read aloud Psalm 23:3 and 25:4-5. Ask them to think about what kinds of challenges make their paths difficult to walk. What do steep hills or blocked pathways represent in their walks with God? What can clear away the debris or make the journey easier? When do they need time to sit and rest and talk with God along their trails? Then, say a prayer that everyone might walk more closely with God.

3. As youth work on the trail, offer encouragement and guidance. If some are unsure of their tasks, show them what to do (clearing a certain section, picking up trash, building a step) and remind them to follow through to completion. Engage the youth in conversations as they work. Remind them what you asked them to think about regarding their individual life paths. Also make sure people take rest and water breaks.

4. When the group is finished working, gather everyone back at the beginning of the path and read aloud again Psalm 23:3 and 25:4-5. Assure the group that you and other leaders in the church community want to serve as "trail guides" in their lives, offering support, guidance, and even helping to clear away the "brush" or "debris" that make following God's path difficult. If any are willing, allow them to talk about some of the thoughts they've had about their journey with God.

5. Close with a group prayer, asking God to guide each person on his or her walk along God's path of righteousness.

Bright Ideas

IDEA

- ☼ If there is not a suitable trail near your community, consider finding an area where you could create a trail. Property along a river or waterway, a nearby park, or even your church property might be great places for people to walk and spend time enjoying nature. If you decide to use your church property, consider designing a "prayer trail" by posting stops with signs along the way for people to offer certain prayers to God, listen for guidance on various topics, and contemplate certain Scriptures.

Destination Unknown Missions 30 Excursions to Transform Your Community

HOME REPAIR

FOCUS

Youth will help with home repairs, developing a working relationship with local service agencies and meeting their neighbors' housing needs.

SCRIPTURES

Deuteronomy 15:11; Psalm 82:1-4

LOCATION

Local homes in need of repair

ABOUT THE DESTINATION

Many youth enjoy doing house repairs, especially when it's work that can be completed in a few hours or days and makes a noticeable difference. Contact an agency in your community that helps people with housing needs and talk to them about the abilities of your group and its desire to participate in some local work. Prior to the work day, take one or two youth with you (and another adult) to meet the homeowner and to assess what kinds of materials and tools you will need.

Plan to take a camera (or use a cell phone camera) and take pictures of the house before and after youth have completed their work.

ON THE WAY

Ask the group to agree on a list of top five things they think makes a house truly a "home" for the people who live there. Talk about the items on the list. Are they actual physical things one might buy, or are they experiences (like memories, love, trust, and safety)? Also, tell youth a little about the family who lives in the home they will repair, and encourage your youth to get to know the homeowner and family during the time they are working.

Preparation

✪ Contact an agency in your community that helps people with housing needs. Communicaste your desire to help on a local project.

✪ Before starting the project, meet with the homeowner to determine the work needed and the necessary tools.

✪ Gather tools and make sure you have enough people available to do the required work, included any adults needed.

✪ Review Deuteronomy 15:11 and Psalm 82:1-4.

Bright Ideas

- ❂ To develop leadership within your group, assign some of your youth to do the legwork for this activity, such as contacting the agencies, talking to the families, and visiting the sites (with adults) to determine the supplies needed for the work.

- ❂ To help develop relationships with adults in your congregation, identify adult volunteers who are familiar with the tools you will use on this job and invite them to join you for this activity. Make sure the adults understand that the youth will be doing the work. The adults' role is to teach and guide, making sure that the youth are safe.

AT THE SITE

1. When you arrive at the site, introduce your team to the homeowner and family. Briefly review with the homeowner the work that needs to be done.

2. Explain the necessary tasks to the group and assign duties to each person. Be careful that those who are using tools (power, sharp, heavy-lifting) are capable of doing such work and are armed with the necessary safety precautions and gear. If they are inexperienced, call on the experienced adults to teach youth how to do the tasks or use the equipment. Be careful not to rush, and encourage the youth to take their work seriously, reminding them that they are working to repair someone's home. They should treat this home better than their own houses.

3. Throughout the work time, remind youth to talk with and get to know the family that lives in this home.

4. When the work is complete, clean up the site and thank the family for allowing you to help. Take pictures, if possible, and invite the family to worship for an upcoming Sunday. Make sure that the family feels welcome and included in your community, but do not pressure them to attend worship or give them the impression that their attendance is expected in return for the work your team accomplished.

5. On the way back to the church, find a place where you and the group can talk about what happened at the worksite. Perhaps you can stop for a cold drink or hot chocolate, depending on the season. Ask:

   - ❂ What happened today that you will remember for a long time? Why?
   - ❂ What did you learn to do today that you didn't know how to do before?
   - ❂ How did God use you today? How did you rely on God today?

   Point out to youth that one of the blessings of working on local houses is that they will be reminded of the work they did every time they pass the house, and they may encounter that homeowner months or even years after the work is completed.

   Also tell the youth that they can continue to work through the agency that helped you connect with this family and explain that process. They do not need to wait for the whole youth group to participate. Individuals who are interested my volunteer.

6. Read aloud Deuteronomy 15:11 and Psalm 82:1-4. Ask how the Scriptures relate to the work you did today. Talk about the follow-up that your group should do so that the people you served today will know that you continue to think about them. What kind of memories have you given them that

will help their house be more of a home? Point out that the physical work completed today will last for only so long. Shingles decay; wood gets old and needs replacing; paint eventually chips and peels. But the love and friendship they shared can last a lifetime, and the memories they keep of that love and service can nurture strong and steadfast faith as God uses the experience to strengthen everyone involved.

7. Close with a prayer, naming the family you served and asking God to bless their home and continue to strengthen everyone involved in the day's event.

Notes

What is it that truly makes a house a home?

Hunger Meal

Focus

Youth will partake in a meal that helps them imagine being in either a "fully developed country" or a "developing country" setting and teaches them about hunger and food insecurity in other parts of the world.

Scripture

Matthew 25:31-46

Location

A place to eat, such as your church's fellowship hall or someone's home

About the Destination

It may seem ironic to use a meal to educate people about world hunger, but the irony is part of why this idea is effective. Each person is invited to enjoy a meal, but only a very few actually will eat a full menu consisting of meat, vegetables, bread, and dessert. Most everyone else will eat the kind of meal indicative of a second- or third-world country (with similar rights and privileges).

One in six Americans struggles with hunger; one in four American children go to bed hungry each day. And more than 16,000 children die from hunger-related causes. According to U.S. Poverty Statistics (*www.bread.org*), half of Americans will live in poverty sometime before they are 65 years of age.

These statistics are only American statistics. Poverty and hunger in the world is similar. Of the estimated 7 billion people in the world, 925 million are hungry. That's about 1 in 7. In poorer countries, though, the ratio is about 1 in 3. Poor nutrition plays a role in at least half of the 10.9 million child deaths each year— 5 million deaths. Research and gather additional information by visiting the websites of organizations such as Bread for the World, The Hunger Project, and UMCOR. Print out some facts about hunger around the world and plan on presenting these facts during the meal. Also print information about organizations that are working to fight hunger and how to contact them. You might present the information by printing the facts and the organizations' contact information on the bottom of placemats or napkins.

Preparation

⚙ Find a location to host your meal.

⚙ Create the menu and purchase the food, along with supplies for table settings.

⚙ Research hunger and poverty and create an information sheet including statistics and ways that youth can help. You might print this information on napkins or placemats.

⚙ Create two posters with the statements provided on page 78. Also obtain a metronome.

⚙ Review Matthew 25:31-46.

There is lots more information to share with your youth, but perhaps the most important is the fact that there is enough food in the world to keep everyone comfortably well-fed. Unfortunately, too much food is wasted and not enough is shared with those who have little or none.

Create a poster that says: *"16,000 children die of hunger-related causes each day. That's one every five seconds."* Create another poster that says: *"I was hungry, and you gave me food to eat."* —Matthew 25:35. Display the first poster in the room where you will eat and near a metronome that beats about once every five seconds. Display the second poster on another wall of the room.

Enlist a team to plan the meal. Organize some volunteers to serve, because the food should be served to the tables where youth sit. Also plan table settings that symbolize the developed and developing countries by using china and flatware for the few (developed) and paper plates, cups, and plastic spoons for the rest. All of the table settings representing the developed countries should be together in one area. You may also wish to place armbands or colored name tags at the appropriate table settings, differentiating between the countries.

Make sure there is enough good food to feed everybody (as there is in the world), but only serve the full meal to one quarter of the group, or those who sit at the nice plates and utensils. Plan to give them plenty of food, serving it in bowls and on platters. The rest of the group (paper plates) should receive only the starchy item from the menu—single servings of rice or potatoes, bread, and some broth would be fine. (You might serve a few people another vegetable, but only limited amounts.) Also, the area representing developed countries should have pitchers of milk, juice, and ice water; youth representing developing countries should receive only water (no ice).

On the Way

Ask those who travel with you to the destination (if you are having the dinner at someone's home or a location other than the church) to tell about a time they remember being hungry. When did they have to go without eating for a long time? Why? It is possible that some in your group have truly experienced poverty and hunger. If so, be sensitive and make sure you express support for those youth.

At the Site

1. Welcome the group before they take their seats and explain that everyone is about to enjoy a special meal. Read aloud the menu, then ask everyone to be seated. Allow the youth to sit wherever they wish. Make sure that none of them are aware of the reason for the difference in place settings.

Bright Ideas

IDEA

- ✪ After the youth have experienced this meal, ask if any would be willing to serve a similar meal to an adult group in the church or community. Your group can increase hunger awareness by teaching others.

2. Tell the group that this meal will help them to learn about world hunger. Explain that some of them will be served all of the food on the menu, but many of them will be served only a small portion of what has been prepared, representing food distribution in the world today. Point out the statistics and information you've provided (on a handout, napkin, or placemat). Also share any other research you gathered ahead of time.

Now explain the difference in the place settings and tell the youth that there are some rules as you go forward with the meal: They can eat only the food that is served to them, and only those representing "developed countries" may move anywhere else in the room. The rest of them must remain seated where their plates have been placed. Remind them to wear their armbands or colored name tags.

3. Say a prayer, offering thanks for the food and the program that has been prepared. Then ask the servers to begin serving the food.

4. As youth begin their meal, watch to be sure that they follow the rules. Remember, only the youth originally seated at a place for developed countries are allowed to move around the room. Also watch to see if any of the youth who were served plenty of food decide to move around and share their food with those who don't have a lot of food. This gesture is allowed, though you should not suggest it to anyone. Let the youth figure it out for themselves. When they do, watch to see that only the people with much are the ones moving from table to table, sharing their plenty with those who have little.

5. When the meal is finished (including dessert), talk about what happened: Who was served? Who received more food? Was the food distributed? Why or why not? Who thought of moving around and giving excess food to someone who had little? How is this meal like the situation in the world today? Who has the wealth? (If they answer "America," you should point out some statistics of poverty in the United States.) How could the food in the world be more equally distributed? Do you know any organizations that work to fight hunger?

6. Call attention again to the fact sheet and talk about ways that youth can participate in the fight to end hunger. Read aloud Matthew 25:31-46 and explain that Jesus calls us to feed the hungry because, by feeding the hungry, we feed him. Emphasize that, if they shared their food during this meal, they were showing what the kingdom of God is like: a place where all people love one another. If God loves all of us, and if we have Christ living in us, then we, too, should be moved to do as Christ would do—to feed the hungry.

7. Close with another prayer, thanking God again for the meal and asking God to help everyone who has much to be more thoughtful and generous toward those who have little.

Notes

Hunger Meal

MEAL DELIVERY

FOCUS

Youth will help prepare and deliver meals to homebound people, giving the youth an opportunity to be the presence of Christ to those they are serving and also to learn about the needs of people in their community who are often overlooked.

SCRIPTURE

Matthew 25:31-45

LOCATION

The homes of homebound persons in your community

ABOUT THE DESTINATION

People who are confined to their homes often struggle with loneliness, depression, and feelings of being forgotten by others. Jesus calls us to care for the sick, even telling us that we will encounter Christ in such visits. Give your youth an opportunity to encounter the Christ in these visits with the homebound in your church and community.

Many communities have a Meals on Wheels program. You can find out if Meals on Wheels exists in your community by doing an online search at *mowaa.org*. If there is a program near you, contact them and ask to take your group for a visit, volunteering to help prepare food and ride along with the volunteers as they deliver the food. If there is not a local Meals on Wheels, contact another agency that helps the needy and volunteer to help them prepare and, if possible, deliver meals for people who need help or are homebound.

Another idea is to talk to your church staff about providing meals for people in your congregation who are homebound and could use some company. If this is the best option for your group, make some calls and arrange a day when you and your youth can deliver warm lunches. Bringing a prepared lunch helps the person you are visiting to know that you have put some thought into the visit. Don't stay too long (you don't want the food to get cold), but don't simply drop off the food and leave, either. Talk with the person for a while, asking if there any other needs your church could meet.

Preparation

- ✪ Research Meals on Wheels in your community at *mowaa.org*.

- ✪ Ask someone on your church staff for a list of members who are homebound.

- ✪ If you are preparing the meals, arrange to use the church kitchen (if there is one) or someone's home; also organize a shopping trip to purchase food.

- ✪ Review Matthew 25:31-45.

While simply driving to a house with youth and, at the last moment, explaining why you're there is a great way to start this activity, you might also begin at the church (or, if your church doesn't have a kitchen, at someone's house) where, as a group, you will prepare the food for the home visits. Talk about the people you are going to visit as you prepare the meals. If your group is large, divide the group into smaller teams of four or five. (Assign two unrelated adults to each team.) Too many people at once can be overwhelming to those you visit.

ON THE WAY

Ask the youth if they know people who are confined to their homes. Encourage them to think about the following: What would they do if they could not get out of the house to buy food or other necessities? What if the only way they could talk to someone was through the telephone or the Internet? What would their relationships be like? What would they miss most?

AT THE SITE

1. As you travel to the first home, remind youth that you are visiting homebound people. Help youth unload the prepared food and take it to the door. Be sure to introduce everyone when you first arrive. Make the visit short (without sitting and watching the other person eat) but meaningful. Here are some questions that might help generate conversation at the start of a visit:

   ❂ How long have you lived in this community?
   ❂ What has changed over the years in this area?
   ❂ Is there anything we (the church) can do to help you in the days or weeks ahead?
   ❂ We'd like to pray for you this week. Do you have any specific prayer needs?

   After praying together, be sure to thank the person for allowing you to visit him or her.

2. Make a few visits with your team. At each stop, encourage the youth to take part in the conversation but also to listen.

3. When you finish your visits, meet all the teams (if there are more than one) back at the church or at someone's home to debrief.

Bright Ideas

❂ If your community does not have a **Meals** on Wheels program, look into organizing some sort of regularly scheduled meal drop-off program for local homebound people. Individuals or groups within your congregation could be in charge of preparing lunches, and intergenerational groups (including at least two unrelated adults) could make the visits and deliver the food.

4. Read aloud Matthew 25:31-45, then ask:

- ⚙ What did you enjoy most about our visits today?
- ⚙ What was difficult about these visits?
- ⚙ Think about the Scripture we read. How did you encounter Christ today?
- ⚙ What did you learn about God's love from this experience?

5. Provide information about how youth can participate in this kind of ministry on a regular basis. Some youth will be happy to organize or join a small group and make monthly homebound visits, either through the church or through a program such as Meals on Wheels.

6. Offer a closing prayer, including a time for youth to speak aloud the names and needs of the people they visited.

Notes

Nursing Home

Focus

Youth will visit a local nursing home or extended-care facility where they will interact with the residents and make themselves available for God's love to be shown through them.

Scripture

Leviticus 19:32

Location

A local nursing home or extended-care facility

About the Destination

Just a century ago it wasn't unusual for a family to include many generations—parents, children, grandparents, and sometimes even great-grandparents lived close to one another, on the same property, or often in the same house. Community gatherings included the young and the old, and children grew up having relationships with the elderly.

Today, though, many of our youth do not spend much time listening to stories told by the elderly; grandparents often don't live in the same city as their children and grandchildren; and schools, churches, and community functions divide people by age categories, separating us from a diversity that could give us strength.

Give your youth an opportunity to talk and listen to older adults. Contact a local nursing home or extended-care facility and make plans to visit for an hour or two. Find out if there are games available (like dominos or bingo) and offer to come and lead a game of bingo for the guests at the facility. Also plan to take an assortment of inexpensive prizes for the winners of each game. Be creative, asking your youth if they would like to volunteer themselves as prizes (singing a solo to a winner, making some sort of craft or picture for a winner, and so on). Also, gather some information about what was happening seventy or eighty years ago: What wars were going on? What products and technologies were being invented and developed? What had not been invented yet? How did teenagers spend their time?

Preparation

- ✲ Contact a local nursing home or extended-care facility and make plans to visit and play games with the residents.

- ✲ Purchase an assortment of inexpensive prizes.

- ✲ Research what was happening in the world seventy or eighty years ago.

- ✲ Review Leviticus 19:32.

ON THE WAY

Ask the youth to think about what life was like seventy or eighty years ago. Be prepared to tell some of the information you gathered ahead of time about life in the past. Ask if they know anyone who is eighty years old or older. What do they like to talk about? What music do they enjoy? What stories do they tell? Tell the youth that at this destination they will meet elderly persons in a nursing home.

AT THE SITE

1. Read aloud Leviticus 19:32.

2. Ask: "Why would God command God's people to take care of their elders? Why are older adults so important to our community? What can we learn from them?"

3. Explain that every person in the group will help one person who lives in the facility to play bingo. Make sure the youth understand that some people will require physical help to play while others will be able to play on their own. The youth should help as necessary and work to create an enjoyable experience for all participants. While they are playing, each youth should learn five things about the person whom he or she is assigned to help and should also tell this person three things about him or herself. Suggest that youth talk to the residents about activities they enjoy, music they like to listen to (or play), what life was like when they were teenagers, or where they grew up and what life was like during that time.

4. Take the youth to the space or room where they will be playing bingo. It may be necessary for some of the youth to help bring folks to the meeting place. When all youth and adults have gathered, introduce your youth and talk about how you are looking forward to spending this time together.

5. Pair up each youth with someone from the nursing home and begin the game. During the game you might need to help youth begin some conversations or to feel more at ease with their partners. Gently remind them of the topics you mentioned earlier: activities, music, life as a teenager, and so on.

6. After about an hour of playing bingo, ask if anyone would like to sing some songs or tell some of the stories they learned from their partners. Allow a little more time for youth and residents to visit, then suggest youth help them return to their rooms, if necessary.

Bright Ideas

IDEA

❂ If this event goes well, schedule monthly or quarterly activities with this nursing home. Relationships are built over time, and helping your youth to get to know some of the older members of their community will benefit everyone involved.

7. When all adults have returned to their rooms, gather the youth together and read aloud again Leviticus 19:32. Then ask:

⊙ What are some things you learned about your partner today?
⊙ What do you have in common with your partner?
⊙ How did the time spent today help you? What did you learn, or how has your perspective changed?

8. Explain that people often find it easy to dismiss the opinions of the elderly and avoid spending time with them. God's Word shows us how seriously we are expected to take the commandment to respect those who are older. The wisdom they share could keep us from making bad decisions.

9. Close by joining hands in a circle, while each person says a short prayer for the elderly person that he or she met and helped today.

Notes

God's Word commands us to respect and value
the wisdom of the elderly.

PRAYER BLANKETS

FOCUS

Youth will meet with a group of adults in the church who will teach them how to make prayer blankets and talk about prayer. When the blankets are completed, the group will pray over them and then make available for pastors and others to hand out to people in need of prayer and comfort.

SCRIPTURES

Philippians 4:6-7; Colossians 1:9-14; 1 John 5:14-15

LOCATION

At someone's home, in a retreat setting, at the church, or at a community center—anywhere you can gather people around tables and spread out blankets

ABOUT THE DESTINATION

In pastoral care situations the pastor often comforts people by assuring them that the community of faith is praying for them. Wouldn't it be helpful on such a visit to give someone a comfortable blanket as a reminder of the "blanket of prayers" being offered up for that individual in need? Some churches already have a prayer blanket ministry. If yours does, contact the leader of that ministry and set up a time when you and your group can meet with and make blankets with those volunteers. If you do not know of such a ministry in your church, ask two or three adult church members who are familiar with sewing or other textile arts to do a little research and prepare a tutorial for your youth on how to make a prayer blanket and how it can be helpful for someone who is ill or homebound. There are a variety of ways to make prayer blankets, some easier than others. Choose a method that will be comfortable for your youth. Resources for making prayer blankets or starting a prayer blanket ministry abound on the Internet.

It is important for this activity to bring in some adults who enjoy sewing, knitting, or crocheting, as this helps develop relationships between the youth and others in the congregation who might not otherwise spend much time together.

Preparation

✪ Find out if your congregation has a prayer blanket ministry. If so, find out how your youth can participate. If not, identify adults in your congregation who can teach the youth how to make blankets.

✪ Research and purchase the necessary supplies.

✪ Review Philippians 4:6-7; Colossians 1:9-14; and 1 John 5:14-15.

ON THE WAY

As you travel to the location where you will be making the blankets, talk to the youth about a time in their lives when they needed assurance that people were praying for them. Ask:

- How does it feel to know that someone is praying for you?
- How does it feel if you think that no one knows about your needs?
- Can you pray for someone without knowing the particulars of his or her struggles?
- What kinds of questions do you have about prayer?"

AT THE SITE

1. Introduce the youth to the adults who have come to help with making the blankets. Explain the impact behind a prayer blanket: The blankets are prayed over by those who make them (as they are making them), and later they are given to people in need as reminders that the community of faith is "covering them in prayer."

2. Allow the adult volunteers to show the youth how to make the blankets. Encourage everyone's involvement. If some don't feel comfortable stitching or cutting, they can offer prayers and conversation alongside someone else who is doing the work.

3. As the youth begin making the blankets (but before they actually start praying over the blankets), read aloud Philippians 4:6-7; Colossians 1:9-14; and 1 John 5:14-15. Ask the youth if they are familiar with any Scriptures related to prayer. What are they? Talk about prayer and how God uses the prayers of others to bring comfort and healing. Youth may struggle with an understanding of prayer, wanting to know why sometimes God doesn't seem to answer prayers. Suggest that God always answers prayers, but often not in the way we want or expect. Ask youth what they think it means to pray for God's will. Point out that Jesus himself asked God to spare him from the cross during his prayer at Gethsemane, but also asked for God's will above all things (see Mark 14:34-36).

   Don't be afraid that youth will raise questions about prayer that you may not be able to answer. We don't understand everything about prayer, but we can come before God with the confidence that God hears our prayers and answers them and that, through prayer, we grow in our relationship with God. Remind youth that the prayers the group offers this day will bring comfort to people who need to feel God's presence with them in days ahead.

4. Make sure you offer some silent time for the youth to pray over the blankets while they are actually making them. Some ministries create fringes along the edges of the blankets and then pray over each knot they tie in the fringes

Bright Ideas

IDEA

- If your church does not have a prayer blanket ministry, ask around to see if there are members of the congregation who would be interested in starting one.

- Another variation on the prayer blankets is "prayer bears." This ministry makes (or purchases) stuffed bears which are prayed over and then given to children who visit a local hospital emergency room.

(prayer knots). Explain that a time of silence is necessary so that people can concentrate on their prayers. Some suggested brief prayers at this time are: *"God, your will be done for the one who receives this blanket,"* or *"God, bring your comfort, your healing, and your presence to the person who receives this blanket."* A breath prayer is also a helpful teaching moment. An appropriate breath prayer would be saying the word *peace* or *comfort* in the tying of each knot.

5. When the blankets are finished, gather the group together and say a prayer over all the blankets, asking guidance and discernment for those who deliver the blankets during times of need.

6. Thank those who volunteered to help with this ministry and then deliver the blankets to a pastor or to someone in charge of visiting the hospitalized or the homebound. Or, you can pile the blankets in the sanctuary for an upcoming worship service, telling the congregation about the activity and how the ministry will bring comfort to people in need.

Prayer blankets are given to people in need
as reminders that the community of faith is
"covering them in prayer."

Notes

Rake and Run

Focus

Youth will travel to several homes of people in the community, quickly raking leaves in the yards, then bagging the leaves and carting them away with no recognition or thanks for their work.

Scripture

Galatians 5:13-14

Location

Nearby residential neighborhoods, specifically yards that need leaves raked and bagged (especially homes of shut-ins or the elderly who cannot do the work themselves)

About the Destination

Imagine looking out your window and seeing a lawn that you expected to be covered in leaves, only to discover it has been freshly raked. The leaves are gone and so are the people who did the work. Obviously they did the work out of kindness and not in an effort to receive any kind of reward.

Help your youth understand the Christian concept of service by hitting the streets one fall afternoon to rake and bag the leaves in nearby lawns. You will need to enlist the help of one or two people with trucks to cart away the leaves, enough rakes for each youth to have one, and lawn bags. Contact a waste disposal company or the city works department to find out where you can deliver the bagged leaves.

Spend some time driving around your neighborhood or areas near your church to determine which streets and yards need the work. Choose an area that appears to have a number of older homeowners who cannot do the yardwork themselves. It also helps to work in a central location (such as a street or a block) so you don't waste time moving from one area to another. Ask permission from the homeowners before doing this work, but don't tell them exactly when you'll show up. Also don't promote your plans to the youth. Simply announce the time, tell the youth to bring work gloves, and begin making a difference in neighbors' lives.

Preparation

✪ Identify a neighborhood with several homes (preferably elderly homeowners) in need of leaf-raking and bagging and ask permission from the homeowners to do this work.

✪ Gather rakes and lawn bags, plan to provide drinking water, and contact someone with a truck you can use to haul away the leaves.

✪ Remind youth to bring work gloves.

✪ Review Galatians 5:13-14.

ADVENTURE

ON THE WAY

Ask the youth what they would do if they discovered that someone did all their chores for them for an entire month? What if they couldn't find out who did their work? How would they thank someone if they didn't know whom to thank?

AT THE SITE

Bright Ideas

IDEA

⊗ Work this destination, along with the "Grocery Store" destination (see page 67), to help youth serve anonymously in their community.

1. When you arrive at the destination, read aloud Galatians 5:13-14. Explain that you and the youth will show love to your neighbors, but will do it without expecting any thanks in return. In fact, you won't even let your neighbors know who did the work.

   Tell the youth that they will be raking yards, bagging the leaves, and then loading the bags into the truck. Encourage them to do a good job and to be very careful not to damage any property (plants, yard lights, and so on). When they finish working in one yard, they should move on to the next. Explain that, if a person whom they are serving comes outside to talk with them, they should be polite and explain that they are doing this work as a way of living out our calling to serve and love one another.

2. As the youth work at raking and bagging, move around the yards and among the workers, offering encouragement and helping when needed. Ask some of the youth if it seems strange doing the work without talking to the homeowners. When a yard is finished, lead everyone in a loud cheer and send them to the next lawn.

3. When youth have finished the yards in the specified area, gather together in a central location. Talk about the work that youth accomplished. How many yards did they complete? Did anyone get "caught" working? What is the reward of doing this work without recognition?

4. Read aloud again Galatians 5:13-14. Explain that Paul, the writer of this letter, wants us to understand that abiding in God's Spirit involves more than our individual faith lives. Personal, spiritual formation is only part of it. As Christians we are called to live out our faith by serving others. Paul reminds us to love our neighbors as we love ourselves, meaning that our love and our faith are wrapped up in our community and in our neighbors.

5. Close this activity with prayer, asking for a different person to pray aloud for each household that you served today.

SANTA'S DAY OUT

FOCUS

Youth will offer service to parents in the community by providing free nursery and childcare on a Saturday so that parents can shop for Christmas gifts and spend a few hours preparing for the holiday season.

SCRIPTURE

1 John 3:16-18

LOCATION

Church nursery

ABOUT THE DESTINATION

This destination is about service to the surrounding community, providing free and safe childcare while parents and other family members shop for Christmas gifts or prepare for the holiday season. Prior to Santa's Day Out, it is important that you get the word out to local neighborhoods. Telling your congregation about this service is not enough. This is an opportunity for the people in your community to learn about and experience God's love through the presence of Christ.

To find out a little more about the parents in your community, visit the United States Census Bureau website, *www.census.gov*, and research statistics for single-parent families in your area. Also find out the number of young children in your area, along with statistics on churched and unchurched families, if possible.

Although you are providing a free childcare service, use this time to provide also an experience that will be fun and demonstrate Christian love for the children. For some of them, this will be the first time they have been inside a church and possibly the first time they have heard the Christmas story. Plan activities that focus on the Christmas story as told in the Gospels of Luke and Matthew.

Make sure to enlist experienced nursery workers on this day. While some of your youth may have logged many hours working in the nursery, it's important to have one adult present for every six or seven children and a minimum of two non-related adults. Plan to accept reservations prior to this day, giving you an opportunity to plan ahead for activities with the children and to enlist sufficient youth and adults to serve.

Preparation

- Research statistical information related to parents and young children in your community at *www.census.gov*.

- Ahead of time publicize your Santa's Day Out in the local neighborhoods.

- Enlist experienced nursery workers, one per every six or seven children.

- Prepare Emergency Health/Information forms to distribute on the day of the event. Make sure you have one of these forms on hand for every child before his or her parents leave.

Also provide emergency health forms for parents to complete about each child. Communicate a clear beginning and ending time for the day so that parents know when they are expected to return and pick up their children.

On the Way

Ask the youth to arrive at least one hour prior to the children so that you can go over the plans for the day, prepare for the activities, discuss the Scripture, and pray for the children, youth, parents, and adult leaders.

At the Site

1. When the youth first arrive, gather in the nursery and ask someone to read aloud 1 John 3:16-18. Then share the statistical information you researched about the children in your surrounding community. Ask, "What kinds of 'truth and action' can we provide today in order to communicate God's love to the children that are coming?" Next, go over the plans for the day, explaining the activities and helping the youth understand that their participation is a response to God's call to be truth and action.

2. As the children arrive, make sure an adult helps with check-in so that parents are assured their children will be safe and that activities are planned for the day. Ask parents to complete the emergency contact forms and ask the parents what time they will return to pick up their children, reminding them of the closing time.

3. Help the youth to stay on task during the day and remind them that their service today is more than simply "babysitting." They are communicating Christ's presence to children who need to experience God's love in action.

4. When the parents or guardians return, thank them for the opportunity to spend time with their children. Tell them a little about the activities you did during the day.

5. When all the children are gone, gather the youth together. Ask them to sit in a circle on the floor or in chairs in the center of the room. Read aloud 1 John 3:16-18 again. Ask the youth to tell about times during the day when they witnessed someone living out John's instructions. Encourage them to think about ways they were the "words and actions" of God's love and to tell about these times. Allow plenty of time for the youth to talk.

6. Close with a prayer, lifting up each child that attended the event, as well as the parents, and asking God to bless the service of each youth and adult who helped during Santa's Day Out.

Bright Ideas

✿ Consider doing a two-week carryover between this activity and the Adopt-A-Child destination (see page 9). Invite the same children to both activities.

✿ Invite a group of core youth to meet prior to this event and plan all the activities for the children. The day will be more meaningful if the youth take ownership of it.

Destination Unknown Missions 30 Excursions to Transform Your Community

STREETS AND SIDEWALKS

FOCUS

Youth will plant trees along the city streets, beautifying their community and creating memories.

SCRIPTURE

Mark 4:14-20

LOCATION

The streets in your community

ABOUT THE DESTINATION

First, contact city works to learn if and where you can plant trees. The space between the street curb and the sidewalk (the "right of way") belongs to the city, but homeowners and businesses are responsible for keeping that area clean and maintained, so check with homeowners and/or businesses connected to that right of way. Make sure everyone approves the planting of trees in that area. You may also want to include them in the choice of trees to be planted.

Once you've decided on the type of trees, visit a local nursery to purchase them and learn about caring for them. Provide enough shovels for the youth to do the digging along with soil and enough water for each planting.

Talk with the adult groups in your church about your plans. They may be willing to donate a particular tree for a particular location. Also, as a part of this activity, contact one or two older adults in your congregation who will speak to the youth about their faith growth. This can be very effective if an older church member, who has lived in the community most of his or her life, can come and talk about some of his or her memories about the neighborhoods.

Review Mark 4:14-20 so that you can supplement information when necessary at the destination site.

Preparation

✪ Contact the appropriate city department to learn if your group can plant trees along the streets in your community.

✪ Purchase trees from a local nursery and collect the tools and supplies you will need to plant and care for the trees.

✪ Invite one or two older members of your congregation to speak to youth about their faith growth.

✪ Review Mark 4:14-20.

ADVENTURE

On the Way

As you drive to the first location where youth will plant a tree, talk with them about some of the things in their lives that have helped their faith to grow. Ask: "What experiences have strengthened your faith? What are the 'fruits' of your faith?"

At the Site

1. Explain that youth will help to beautify their community by planting trees that can be enjoyed by passersby for generations to come. Tell the youth that the trees they will plant are much like the faith that God plants in them. When their faith is nurtured, it also grows and beautifies the world around them.

2. Read aloud the parable from Mark 4:14-20. Spend a few minutes talking about the meaning of this parable. Jesus explained that the seeds planted by the sower (God) are God's Word. They are planted with the intention that they will grow and mature. But not all do. Likewise, God has planted seeds of faith within us. When we nurture our faith through the habits of Bible study, worship, prayer, and acts of mercy and justice, it grows. But if we don't nurture our faith and rely entirely on occasional spiritual experiences such as retreats, church camps, or worship services, it can quickly dry up, like seeds planted in rocky soil. Also, if we are too focused on other things in life, we may not even recognize God's Word when it comes to us, and our faith will be like seeds that are strangled by thorns.

Ask the youth to think about their individual faith seeds as they plant the trees. While digging holes for the roots of the trees to grow deep, they should ask themselves if they are nurturing their faith so that those roots grow deep as well.

3. Based on what you learned at the nursery when you purchased the plants, demonstrate for youth how to plant the trees. Provide shovels, water, and soil for each planting team. Tell the groups where to meet after they have planted all their trees.

4. When the groups have finished planting their trees and you have gathered together again, ask the youth to talk about how their work relates to the parable that you discussed earlier. If some youth need to be reminded of the parable, ask other youth to relate it from memory. Ask one person to tell the parable as far as possible, then ask someone else to take over the story. When youth are finished, add any missing facts, and ask the question again, "How did today's planting relate to this parable?" Then talk about the following:

   ❂ How deep are your roots? Where have your seeds been planted?
   ❂ What can make your life "good soil" for the seeds that God plants?

Bright Ideas

IDEA

❂ Contact the community newspaper to report how your group is helping to beautify the area. Ask them to include an article in the paper or on the paper's website to motivate other groups in your community to also help in its beautification.

✪ What is going on in your life right now that is making a "pathway," or that is creating "rocky" or "thorny" soil?

5. Ask for volunteers to water the newly planted trees in the weeks ahead. Record their names and call them in a few days to remind them of their responsibility.

6. Close by joining hands and offering a prayer, asking God to help youth take care of the seeds planted in their lives, and the lives of others, so that the faith of their friends and neighbors grows in good soil.

Notes

If we nurture the trees we plant with water and sunshine, they will grow. If we nurture our faith through the habits of Bible study, worship, prayer, and acts of mercy and justice, it will grow.

Vacant Lot

Focus

Youth will talk about renewal and transformation as they travel to a vacant lot in the community and spend time cleaning up the property and planting trees, shrubs, and flowers.

Scripture

Genesis 1:1–2:4; Psalm 24:1; 148

Location

A vacant lot in your community that needs some upkeep and cleaning

About the Destination

Drive around your community looking for a lot that needs a "makeover." This lot can be either public or private; though if it were public, more people would be able to appreciate and use it after the work is complete. Contact city officials, informing them of your intent for the lot identified or ask if they have another piece of property that your group might work to beautify. Once the location is chosen and you have received permission to do the work, decide what kind of beautification your group can afford to do (in terms of time, money, skills, and other resources). If your budget is low, then cleaning and mowing may be all you can do. But if you are more ambitious, consider soliciting donations from members of your congregation. Also promote your idea to people in the surrounding area and allow them to donate money or contribute supplies. You might also contact area nurseries and ask for donations of flowers, shrubs, trees, and other plants. Businesses might be willing to contribute in exchange for your promotion about their donations to the project.

Decide on and collect the tools you will need (shovels, clippers, a lawn mower, paintbrushes, paint, rags, drop cloth, and so forth). Be sure youth know to bring work gloves and to dress appropriately for the type of work they will do. If the work will take up most of the day, enlist some church members to bring snacks or lunches for the hungry workers.

Plan to bring along Bibles or printed copies of Psalm 148 to read as a closing liturgy.

Preparation

- Contact city officials or the property owner about ways you can beautify a vacant lot in your community.

- Gather the necessary equipment for the work you will do.

- Enlist church members to provide snacks and/or lunches and drinks.

- Optional: Purchase a recording of the song "Beautiful Things" by Gungor.

- Bring Bibles or printed copies of Psalm 148.

- Review Genesis 1:1–2:4; Psalm 24:1; and Psalm 148.

ON THE WAY

Ask the youth to tell about a time when they experienced renewal or transformation. Be ready to share a personal story of renewal first, if necessary. What caused the change? How did the transformation make things better? Remind the youth that God brings transformation. Tell the Creation Story in your own words (from Genesis 1:1–2:4), pointing out how God brings order from chaos.

AT THE SITE

Bright Ideas

● Does your church property need some beautification? Developing a side lot or spare acreage and making it more accessible will invite people to visit your church and help people to relax and enjoy the property.

● Is there a city park that needs some fresh mulch, weeded gardens, repainted signs and curbs, or repaired playground equipment? Even trimming hedges and grass can revive a rundown city park.

● Invite church members or people who live in the area where you will be working to join in the project.

● On your way to the site or while working, play the song "Beautiful Things" by Gungor. Point out the lyrics, which praise God for bringing beauty out of chaos.

1. Begin your time by reading aloud Psalm 24:1 to the group. Tell the youth about the work they will be doing on the property. Talk about how God can take something that is broken and dirty and transform it into something beautiful. Explain that your group will be God's agents of transformation today. They will give a vacant lot a makeover, turning something that was neglected and abandoned into something beautiful.

2. Encourage the youth as they work. Give each person specific tasks and clear goals. Explain how each completed task contributes to the beauty of the lot. Take plenty of breaks and provide water so that everyone stays hydrated.

3. When the work is finished, gather the youth together in a central part of the property and look at all you have accomplished. Point out how each person contributed to the beautification, naming which people did what work. Explain that God used them to make something beautiful for the community.

4. Ask the youth to think of areas in their lives that are broken or that need to be reclaimed by God. Explain that God often brings beauty and hope to the dusty, dried-up parts of our lives and brings order to those parts that are in chaos. Though God is responsible for such transforming work, we can participate. The first step is for us to offer the broken parts of our lives to God and then trust God to turn them into something beautiful.

5. Allow the youth to spend some silent time with God. Instruct them to find a space where they worked on the property and to sit there quietly. Encourage them to reflect on their lives and to think about how God is present in those parts of their lives that need to be transformed. Invite them to offer their brokeness to God in prayer.

6. After a few minutes, call for youth to regroup. Hand out Bibles or printed copies of Psalm 148. Read Psalm 148 as a responsive reading: A leader should read aloud the first verse; everyone else should respond by reading aloud the second verse. Continue alternating verses until you have read the entire psalm. Then close in prayer, asking God to remind us all of the beautiful things God has planned for creation.

VISIT HOMEBOUND PERSONS

FOCUS

Youth will spend some time with shut-ins and homebound persons who live in your community, getting to know them and their stories while telling a little about themselves, too.

SCRIPTURE

Leviticus 19:32; 1 Timothy 5:1-2

LOCATION

Homes of people in the community who are unable to get outside because of physical or emotional hardship

ABOUT THE DESTINATION

Scripture repeatedly calls us to care for the elderly. Leviticus 19:32, for example, tells us to "respect the elderly," and the early church in Acts appointed seven new apostles, specifically so that they could make sure that widows (many of them elderly) were shown care and concern. Today's youth seldom find themselves in settings where they spend time getting to know elderly persons in their community. Even at church we tend to separate youth from the rest of the body of Christ, limiting the wisdom of older generations that is available for our young people.

Contact your church office to find about people in your congregation and/or community who aren't able to leave their homes very often, perhaps because of a physical or emotional hardship. Schedule a time when several of your youth, along with two adults, can visit with these folks. Prepare a separate note card for each person/home youth will visit, listing the name and address of the person, along with any information that might be helpful (such as whether the person is hard of hearing, takes a long time to answer the door, lives with one of his or her adult children, and so on). Don't plan on visiting too long, but do plan on taking flowers or fruit to each person visited.

Also purchase a thank-you card for each household you will visit, envelopes for mailing the cards, and stamps.

Preparation

- Identify homebound persons in your congregation and/or community and make arrangements to visit them.

- Prepare note cards listing important information such as whether persons you plan to visit are hard of hearing, take a long time to get to the door, and so on.

- Purchase fruit or flowers, a thank-you card, and stamps for each person you plan to visit.

- Review Leviticus 19:32; 1 Timothy 5:1-2.

Bright Ideas IDEA

✪ Ask your pastor (or other pastoral staff member) to come along with your group to this destination. He or she has experience visiting the homebound, and it is a great way for one or two youth to observe the pastor in a setting other than a worship service.

On the Way

As you travel to the homes of the shut-in, ask the youth if they've ever spent much time with people over eighty years of age. Ask them to tell who and in what circumstances. What do they know about these people's stories? What did they learn from them?

Explain that up until the mid-twentieth century many people lived with or very near to their grandparents, and it was quite common for young people to eat meals and attend gatherings with the elderly. Today, however, youth don't spend much time with people from older generations.

At the Site

1. When you arrive at the gathering location (whether it will be the first home to visit, the church, or a meeting place in the community), tell everyone that they will be forming small teams of two or three youth and two adults (for safety purposes) and then visiting people who are homebound. Ask if anyone can explain the term *homebound*. Talk about the meaning of the term (see following page), then read aloud Leviticus 19:32 and 1 Timothy 5:2. Tell the group that God's Word often directs us to care for those in older generations.

2. Divide the youth into small teams of two or three, along with two adults. Agree on a time and place where teams will return to talk about their visits. Remind the groups that it is important to be courteous and respectful. If there are any instructions about particular households, communicate them now, then hand out the cards with specific information to each team. Finally, pray with the teams, asking God to bless and be present with the teams and the persons visited.

3. When youth and adults return to the specified place, ask them to sit together in their visitation teams. Move around and ask each team to tell a little about its visit. Teams don't need to go into detail about their conversations, but they should talk about how they felt before the visits and tell something they learned from the visits.

4. Reread Leviticus 19:32 and 1 Timothy 5:1-2, then ask:

   ✪ Why do you think God tells us to care for the elderly and the sick?
   ✪ How were the visits today helpful for the persons you visited? How were they helpful for you?

5. Hand out thank-you cards, envelopes, and pens or pencils for teams to write short notes to the people they visited. Instruct the youth to tell the recipients of the cards that they are thankful for the time they could spend together and that they will pray for them in the days ahead. Then ask the teams to place the cards in the envelopes, address the envelopes, and give the cards to you.

6. Close by placing all the cards in a pile and asking youth to stand in a circle around them. Pray for those whom your youth visited, thanking God for them and asking for their comfort and strength. Also, thank God for your group's willingness to visit and share God's love with others.

> home•bound (hom' bound') *adj.* Restricted or confined to home.

Notes

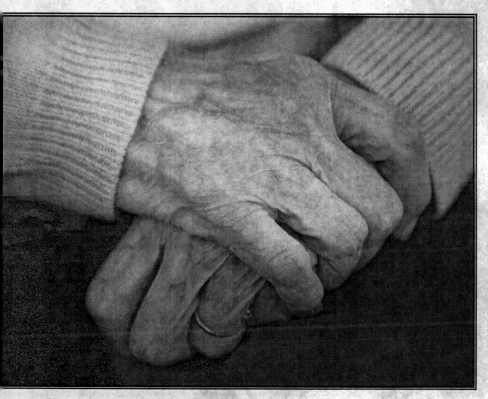

Scripture repeatedly calls us to care for the elderly.

Destination Unknown Missions 30 Excursions to Transform Your Community

Window Washing

Focus

Youth will serve at a gas station, offering to wash peoples' car windows for free.

Scripture

John 13:34

Location

A local gas station

About the Destination

It's a small service to clean someone's windows, but it's a way to show Christian love to a neighbor and most likely will be an act remembered as recipients continue on their way, peering through windows that you and your group washed.

Locate and contact a corner gas station and ask permission for you and your group to approach customers and offer to wash their windows for free. Explain that your youth want to serve, showing love to the community, in this way.

Purchase rags, squirt bottles, and window cleaner. Squeegees are also helpful but not necessary. Prepare a sign that reads "Free Window Washing—Really!" This is important because some drivers will not allow you to clean their windows, thinking that you will expect some sort of tip.

If possible, obtain a recording of the hymn, "They'll Know We Are Christians by Our Love." This song has been recorded by many artists, but one recording that works well is by Jars of Clay. It is also an easy song to play on guitar, if you have someone who plays, or to sing without accompaniment.

If you have enough youth, station a few at the corner to offer the service to people who are in cars stopped at the intersection.

ON THE WAY

As you drive to the gas station, talk about why it's important that our actions show others the love of Christ. Ask the the following:

- ❂ How do people know that you are a Christian?
- ❂ What have you done in the past week or month that has let people know that you follow Christ?

Bright Ideas

- ❂ If possible, provide this service on the same corner as the "Free Lunch" service (see page 59). People will remember the grace you've shown them whenever they drive through this intersection.

AT THE SITE

1. Play (or have someone sing) the song "They'll Know We Are Christians by Our Love" and then read aloud John 13:34. Explain that Jesus gave us this commandment because this is the heart of God—a heart of love. If we have God's Spirit in us, then we, too, will have a heart of love and love one another.

2. Ask: "What does God's love look like? What are some characteristics of God's love?"

3. Explain to the group the service they will be performing. Hand out the spray bottles and rags (or buckets and squeegees). Make it clear to everyone that they should *not* accept donations or tips. Youth may say where they are from (your church name), but it is important that people know that there are no ulterior motives behind this service; it's simply an opportunity to show love to your neighbors.

4. Work for an hour or more with your youth. As you work, spend some time talking with the customers. It could lead to opportunities to invite them to visit your church.

5. When you have finished working, gather everyone together and go to a place where you can talk about what happened. Ask:

- ❂ How did your work today show people Christ's love?
- ❂ Why, do you think, did some people turn down our service?
- ❂ Which, do you think, was easier for them, allowing you to serve or turning you down? Why?

6. Reread John 13:34. Ask the youth how they will show Christ's love to strangers this week. Then close with a prayer, offering up the work you have done and asking that God take what you did and make it meaningful for those with whom you were in contact.

Day Camp for Kids

Focus

Youth will organize and carry out a weeklong day camp for area children, connecting with Jesus' instructions to have faith like children.

Scripture

Matthew 18:1-4

Location

Your church or a community center where you can plan and hold a summer day camp for children

About the Destination

Helping your youth plan and direct a summer day camp can have a positive impact on the children in a community. Such a day camp offers many opportunities throughout the course of a week: It helps develop relationships between your youth and the children; it creates an environment for Christ to be introduced and experienced by children and youth; and it can bring together children from diverse backgrounds and economic situations, breaking down walls that might otherwise divide the people in our communities.

Before beginning to plan with your youth, decide if the camp will be held at your church or another community location. If not at your church, contact the appropriate people to reserve the space.

Most of the work for this camp will take place during the planning. Encourage your youth to take the lead, pointing out that their leadership in this event now will help mold them into community leaders for the future. The culmination of it all, though, is a fun-packed week of outreach to area children, allowing your youth to experience the kingdom of God while nurturing the faith of children. Help your youth claim that vision for their week.

Make sure your leaders and youth are trained in your denomination's (or church's) safety policy for working with children. While your church may not require special training for youth under age 18, it will be helpful for them to attend a training session to prepare them for the responsibilities of working with children.

Preparation

- Decide on a location for your day camp.

- Write the words "Faith Like a Child" across the top of a large sheet of paper and provide markers for youth.

- Use the suggestions on pages 110-112 to plan the camp. Purchase and organize supplies for the week. Contact businesses who can help with supplies, food, and other resources.

- Determine youth responsibilities for setting up and running the camp (see page 111). Make sure leaders and youth are trained in a safety policy.

- Review Matthew 18:1-4.

ADVENTURE

On the Way

As you drive to the location of your summer camp (if not at your church), talk with your youth about their childhood memories. Ask questions such as:

Bright Ideas

IDEA

○ Schedule this event shortly after the Children's Carnival destination (see page 27). Invite the families who attend the carnival to also attend the camp.

◉ Where did you grow up?
◉ Who were your friends?
◉ When did you get involved in a church? Did the church you attended (maybe it was this one) ever have a day camp? If so, what did you do there?
◉ Whom, at church, did you admire?

At the Site

1. Read aloud Matthew 18:1-4. Explain that Jesus told his followers that there is something about children that we should emulate when it comes to our faith. Being like children helps us better experience God's kingdom. Ask, "What is it about childlike faith that Christ wants us never to lose?" Hand out markers and ask youth to write answers on the "Faith Like a Child" chart you prepared ahead of time.

2. Ask, "What can we learn about faith from our children?" Talk about answers that youth wrote on the chart. Explain that you want them to experience childlike faith and to witness the kingdom of God right here in the neighborhood. Tell the youth that they will reach out to area children by planning, promoting, and directing a day camp. Talk for a few minutes about the impact that this camp can have on the children in the community and the responsibility that you and the youth accept by taking on this project. Lead a prayer asking for wisdom and guidance as you plan for the camp in the days ahead. Also begin praying now for the children who will attend and their families.

3. Begin planning the camp by making decisions about the following factors:

   ◉ <u>For how many days of the week will the camp run and during what times each day?</u> Will parents be required to bring children the whole week, or can they choose individual days to participate?
   ◉ <u>What will be the dates of the camp?</u> Think about how much time you need for promotion and implementation.
   ◉ <u>What will be the theme of the camp?</u> It is best to choose a scriptural theme, so that the children will learn faith lessons. Possible themes include Jesus' parables, growing seeds of faith, healings, amazing miracles, creation and me, and serving others. You might even adapt some of the destinations in this book as service opportunities each day for the children, using the theme of "Destination Service."

4. Once you have decided on a theme, brainstorm possible activities for each day of the camp. At this point, talk in generalities and record all the ideas. Then, keeping in mind your transportation and time constraints, the ages and interests of the children you will be serving, and your theme, decide which of all the potential activities will work best for your camp.

5. Now that you're decided on the activities you will offer, plan each day's schedule. Make sure to build in time for rest and breaks, since young children need some down time and personal time.

6. Next focus on supplies and budget. Since this is a service to your community, try to offer the day camp free of charge. Think about businesses and people you can approach to help fund the camp. Talk with area agencies about grants, businesses about donations, and Sunday school classes or adult groups in your church about donations and volunteers. If you are going to serve food each day (at least a snack), then talk with grocery stores and restaurants about how they might be able to help. Assign a team of youth to be responsible for organizing a plan for collecting supplies, resources, food, and donations.

7. Assign teams of youth to be responsible for everything you have planned. Here are some planning team suggestions:

   ◎ Promotion: How will you advertise the camp? Consider promoting it with signs and fliers, in newspapers and newsletters, in the church bulletin or on the church projection screen during worship, and on the church website.
   ◎ Donations and supplies: Talk with potential sponsors, whether local businesses and agencies or Sunday school classes and adult groups in your church, about sponsoring your camp and/or donating supplies. Be sure to give credit to your sponsors and also tell the parents of the children who attend which local businesses and agencies contributed.
   ◎ Setup: Set aside at least one day for setup before the camp starts.
   ◎ Transportation: Make sure you have certified drivers and permission forms from the parents or guardians of each participating child.
   ◎ Teaching and lessons: Plan for crafts and learning activities. (Members of this team should talk with the person who oversees children's ministry at your church.)
   ◎ Food: Enlist helpers to prepare and clean up after snacks and meals.
   ◎ Music: Find and prepare songs that youth can teach to children. Decide who will lead the songs and whether accompaniment will come from live instruments or recorded music.
   ◎ Tech: Will you need computers, projectors, sound equipment, or other audiovisual technology?

Notes

○ <u>Emergency contact information, permission forms, release forms, child information forms, and so on:</u> Create and duplicate copies of every necessary form. Make sure several youth are available to help parents complete and gather the forms on the first day they attend camp.

8. Schedule a few more weekly planning meetings. At each meeting (including this first one), ask:

    ○ How do you expect to experience God's kingdom through the children you serve during the camp?
    ○ How can your faith become more like a child's?

Close this meeting with a prayer, asking God to guide the teams and to bless the children who will attend the camp.

9. During the camp, remind the youth often of their vision: to witness childlike faith in those they are serving. At the end of each day, after the children are gone, ask the youth:

    ○ What examples of childlike faith did you observe today?
    ○ In what ways did a child show God's love today?
    ○ What could you do tomorrow that will help you and a child experience the kingdom of God?

10. When the camp concludes, make sure you and your team write letters of thanks to those who helped support the project, including church members, area businesses, and parents of the children who attended.

Notes

WeekLong Mission Camp

Focus

Youth will participate in a weeklong, intense mission camp, sleeping and living in a local church or camp setting, and serving together through local agencies, while connecting to meaningful locations and establishing memories and relationships with those they serve.

Scripture

Luke 10:25-37; Matthew 10:5-8

Why a Local Mission Camp?

In telling the story of the good Samaritan (see Luke 10:25-37), Jesus gave us an example of loving our neighbor as we love ourselves. In the story the injured man on the side of the road was ignored by the priest and the Levite, who were hurrying along to other commitments. Though the injured man was Jewish, the person who finally stopped to help him was a Samaritan. To Jesus' Jewish audience, a Samaritan was the least likely person to stop and help. Jews and Samaritans had a mutual animosity toward each other. They shared a common heritage, but disagreed on which group was the true descendent of the people of Israel and whether the true Temple of God was located in Jerusalem or on Mt. Gerazim. But the Samaritan had compassion on the injured man and stopped what he was doing in order to help and, thus, made an impact on the man's life.

Are you more like the Samaritan or the priest and Levite? Does your ministry serve the people you walk or drive past on a daily basis, or does it ignore these people in favor of outreach efforts made outside of your city, state, or country? How is your youth ministry responding to the hurting people of your community whom God places in your path? Does your group rely on others from another town or country to do missions in your city while your youth travel somewhere else?

The good Samaritan carried the injured man to an inn. But the Samaritan didn't stop there. He made sure that the man would be cared for physically, and he promised to return to check on his well-being. He began a relationship with the man he helped. Youth can't help but connect with the people they work alongside and the people they serve. But too often, after the mission experience is over, youth have little or no contact with the people they met while serving.

Preparation

- Contact a local homeless shelter, a food bank, or a soup kitchen and volunteer your youth, in small groups, for one to two hours of service.

- Review the service destinations offered in this resource.

- Pray, and pray some more. Then follow the preparation steps provided on pages 116-120.

- Review Luke 10:25-37; Matthew 10:5-8.

A local mission camp for youth will teach participants about the needs of people around them; it will help build the leadership skills of the youth who lead the program; it will initiate relationships with people they meet for the first time, and it will solidify those relationships as they continue to grow in the years ahead. A local mission camp introduces youth to agencies and organizations close to home, allowing them to continue reaching out in service and compassion long after the camp concludes.

There will be many questions as your group begins to plan the mission camp: Will the camp be open to other local youth groups? What local organizations and agencies will be involved? How will you identify the needs you want to meet in the community? Who will speak during the worship times? What type ministry could interest youth to want to stay and serve people in their own city? How does one plan a camp like this? What is the timeline for preparation and promotion? Will participants go home each night or stay at the campsite? How will you feed everyone?

Read this article and then spend time in prayer and reflecting on how God may be calling you to serve your community. There's nothing wrong with going away to help others. Taking youth out of their comfort zone is important; it helps us focus on God's strength and provision in an unfamiliar situation. But showing youth how to be comfortable in serving the needs of those closest to them is a vital part of living out our call in God's kingdom.

Bright Ideas
IDEA

⚙ Consider inviting other church youth groups to participate in your camp. The more hands you have, the more help you can give. Also additional registration fees will allow the group to accomplish more work.

GETTING TO KNOW THE NEIGHBORS

In Luke 10 a lawyer approaches Jesus looking for answers. He first asks Jesus a very basic question, "What must I do to gain eternal life?" (verse 25). (Don't we ask that question again and again even today?) Jesus then turns the question back on the man, "What is written in the Law?" (verse 26). (After all the man is a lawyer; he should know the law.) "Do this and you will live," Jesus says (verse 28).

The man wants to save face, so he asks Jesus the question that leads to the well-known story of the good Samaritan: "And who is my neighbor?" (verse 29). The lawyer doesn't want to let Jesus off the hot seat so easily. Luke says that the man asked the question because he wanted to justify himself. *THE MESSAGE* describes the lawyer as "looking for a loophole" (verse 29).

When it comes to reaching out to our neighbors, the church body continues to look for loopholes. In telling the parable of the good Samaritan, Jesus taught us that anyone in need is our neighbor. But, too often, we have interpreted that teaching as instruction to look past our actual physical neighbors—those in our local community—and reach out to people who live further away.

While mission projects in other states and countries are helpful and, while God often leads us to reach out to strangers in strange lands, let's be careful not to miss the neighbors we pass by on our way out of town. Mother Teresa said, "It

is easy to love the people far away. It is not always easy to love those close to us." What are we teaching our youth about outreach and serving others if their most powerful experiences are with people they'll never see again? What are we witnessing to our community if we are constantly serving people far away rather than the nearby neighbors who need us, too? It may be that our "loophole" allows us to keep both those we serve far away at arms length and those in our community who need us waiting in the ditch.

Whom do your youth consider to be their "neighbors"? Have you asked the youth? Do your youth see the needs in their city or county? Do they know the needs of people across the street or across town? Are there certain areas in the community where they've never been? If they won't go there, then chances are they don't know the needs of many of their neighbors.

Staying Close to Home

In Matthew 10 Jesus sends out his twelve disciples to spread the news that the kingdom of God is imminent. Take a look at Jesus' instructions for their mission:

> Don't begin by traveling to some far-off place to convert unbelievers. And don't try to be dramatic by tackling some public enemy. Go to the lost, confused people right here in the neighborhood. Tell them that the kingdom is here. Bring health to the sick. Raise the dead. Touch the untouchables. Kick out the demons. You have been treated generously, so live generously.
> —Matthew 10:5-8 (*THE MESSAGE*)

Jesus tells his disciples to look for and get to know the lost, confused people who live close to home. He urged them to teach these people that the kingdom is here, to meet their needs, and to relieve their fears.

Do your youth know the lost and confused in the neighborhood? Do the lost and confused in your neighborhood experience Jesus reaching out to them? Who are Jesus's hands in your community? How powerful would it be, for both the recipients and the youth, if he used the hands of your youth?

When choosing a location for a service project, look for a place where youth will experience some discomfort. It helps to take them out of their comfort zone and immerse them in another culture. That's why mission trip locations are often someplace far away—a place with different traditions, a different landscape, different people, and needs that might surprise the youth. (These locations also offer different sites to see, different climates to enjoy, and different activities to try on a day off.)

But you need not go far away in order for your youth to experience the unexpected or to get them out of their comfort zone. Chances are that there are neighborhoods nearby (across the street even?) where your youth will find themselves uncomfortable. They may be surprised to learn that people who live

Notes

Notes

within walking distance live a very different lifestyle and face very different day-to-day challenges. The people whom the youth serve and work alongside may seem like strangers at first. But they are also people whom the youth are likely to see again and again in the grocery store, on the street, in the library, or at school.

Serving in your community isn't easy. You're never truly finished and you never get to leave. It challenges you to establish long-term relationships that will demand time and energy. But instead of dwelling on the challenges, focus on the blessings: How cool is it that Christ will continue using you to reach out to neighbors? How cool is it to develop new relationships and friendships that have the potential to last for many years?

It may not be easy to sell the idea of a local mission camp to your youth. They will likely think a trip to another state or country to be more exciting. Consider offering two mission opportunities: one local and one far away, or a local camp one year and a long-distance location the next.

Opening Their Eyes

However you decide to implement a local mission camp, one of your first steps is opening youths' eyes to the needs in your community. For youth to truly show God's love to their neighbors, they must first see with their eyes and hear with their ears the challenges their neighbors face. They must learn how to listen and how to observe. They must discern need, notice injustice, and recognize poverty and helplessness. They need to open themselves to how God can use them to spread the good news of God's kingdom to their community. While it may be easy to point out (and even respond to) headline-making disasters around the world, it's often difficult to recognize crises just around the corner.

Before planning your camp, visit a few local agencies with the youth. Contact a homeless shelter, a food bank, or a soup kitchen in your area. Review some of the destinations offered in this book and take small groups to visit those locations for an hour or two of service. God is already working through agencies and organizations in your community, so show your youth how to use those resources. Once youth become aware of the man hurting on the side of the road, they'll begin to see ways they can help. They'll learn to respond in a way that is helpful and compassionate, living out the love of Christ to their nearby neighbors. They'll hear Christ's call to stop and get to know their neighbors in need.

Local Mission Camp: Outline for a Year

It is necessary that you begin planning for your local mission camp at least a year in advance. Staying in your community to do mission outreach requires preparation for everyone who will be involved. And the first person you'll need to prepare is you, as leader.

Destination Unknown Missions 30 Excursions to Transform Your Community

Following is a one-year planning outline that will help you and your planning team to stay on task.

One Year or More Before the Event

⊛ **Pray for God's guidance as you choose your group's next mission experience.** While the decision to remain in town and offer this local camp is a good one, God may be calling your group to engage in mission in another way.

⊛ **Get a group of leaders together—both youth and adults—for a time of prayerful discernment.** Ask these leaders to list memorable moments from past mission experiences. How did they use their God-given gifts? What needs did they meet? How did they make an impact on the people and community they served? Then ask them to think about how they might apply their gifts and experience to meet needs in your community. Allow time for prayer and discussion to discern whether God is calling your group to stay home or go elsewhere.

⊛ **Determine a date for the camp.** If you discerned that God is leading and equipping you to plan a local missions camp, check the church calendar, local school calendars, and the schedules of agencies in your community that you would like to involve. You will need the help of as many volunteers as possible, so make sure that there are no other scheduled large church events to compete with your camp.

⊛ **Determine the location.** Even though the camp is local, it is best if youth spend each night at the camp facility. You will need a place where youth can sleep, shower, eat, play, and worship. If one location can accomodate all of these needs, then you've found your place. If all these needs cannot be met at one place, consider what you can do without. For example, though it would be best if there were access to a kitchen, enlisting volunteers to bring already prepared food is an option. If the weather is good and there is room, you can create outside showers using PVC pipe, shower heads, tarps, framework, and access to a hot-and-cold water source.

⊛ **Share your vision and get the support of the youth and their parents.** You should have people in support of this decision before you announce your plans to the congregation. Supporters can help spread your vision to those who raise the question, "Why aren't we going someplace exciting this year?"

⊛ **Determine which destinations in this book you will use as a part of your camp** and get an early start at talking to local agencies about work opportunities during the week of your camp. Working through various local social agencies is key to a successful local mission camp. It is important for your youth to become familiar with local opportunities to serve. You want youth to grow and become leaders in your community, reaching out and serving where the needs are evident.

Notes

Notes

◎ **Enlist adult leaders to be responsible for these areas:**

1. <u>Overseeing the worksites</u>: assessing what work needs to be accomplished, how much work can be finished in a week's time, and what supplies will be needed. These adults also will be responsible for assigning the youth work teams and tending to the worksites during the week.

2. <u>Overseeing the food</u>: planning meals and snacks, enlisting volunteers to prepare and serve the food

3. <u>Quartermaster</u>: accumulating work tools and supplies, making sure the work teams keep these tools and supplies clean and that all supplies and tools are returned to whomever lent them out for the week

4. <u>Overseeing development</u>: procuring food donations from local restaurants, building supplies from hardware stores, and scholarship donations for youth who need financial help

5. <u>Registrar</u>: keeping records of youth who have registered, permission and emergency health forms, and payments

◎ **Determine the cost of the camp for each participant.** Figure how much money you will need to charge participants so that your week breaks even—then charge a little more, if possible. Any money remaining after all bills are paid can be donated to one or spread among all of the agencies who participated in the camp.

◎ **Organize a design team made up of older youth and a few adults.** During the next few monthly meetings, this team should determine:

1. Rules for the camp

2. A camp schedule

3. A camp logo and T-shirt design

4. A camp theme, perhaps using a key Scripture

5. A daily devotional, perhaps a booklet including daily readings written by members of the congregation

6. A dinner night during the week, including parents as well as the people with whom youth are serving and working

7. A guest list, after determining if the camp will be only for your congregation's youth, or will include other groups from your community

8. Promotion

Destination Unknown Missions 30 Excursions to Transform Your Community

Six Months Before the Event

○ **Enlist guest speakers.** Consider inviting a guest each night to visit and speak to your youth. Ask agency representatives, church members involved in service, the senior pastor, and even some of the people with whom you will be serving and working. This is a time for the youth to hear community stories.

○ **Organize worship.** Nightly community worship is important when a group of people gather to serve. It is essential for youth to have time with God and the opportunity to reflect on the day's experiences and times they felt God's presence. You need not determine the content of the nightly worship at this point, but you should decide the type of music you want, who will perform the music, if you need a projector or other equipment, the space or spaces you will use and set up, and who will present the message each night. Pay particular attention to the last night of the camp, since this final worship time can be very powerful.

○ **Organize transportation.** Enlist drivers and vehicles to transport work teams to and from the sites each day as well as to evening activities located separate from where youth are sleeping.

Four Months Before the Event

○ **Make sure that all the necessary materials have been secured and all the necessary arrangements are in place** to lead any of the destinations you have chosen from this book.

○ **Communicate the registration deadline to all your youth.**

Two Months Before the Event

○ **Confirm all commitments from volunteers and donors.**

○ **Identify youth or adult volunteers assigned to each of the following jobs** (and any others that will be necessary for your camp):

1. Photographer

2. Sound and media director

3. Small-group discussion leader

○ **Visit the worksites again,** making sure nothing has changed.

○ **Compile a final list of participants.**

Notes

Notes

○ **Send a letter or an e-mail to the parents of everyone who has registered,** explaining what youth should bring, the rules of the week, and the schedule (including sign-in and pick-up times).

One Month Before the Event

○ **Ask the congregation to pray for the event.** Make sure the congregation is aware of the dates for the camp and ask for prayers and support for preparation time and for the week of the camp.

○ **Arrange for any tools and building supplies you will need to be delivered** prior to the first day of work.

○ **Collect the cell phone numbers of each adult assigned to a worksite.** If an adult doesn't have access to a cell phone, find one that he or she can borrow for the week. Communication is important.

One Week Before the Event

○ **Confirm all commitments from volunteers and donors.**

○ **Rest.** Take some time for yourself before everything begins, so that you are not tired when you start.

○ **Obtain some cash for payments.** There are some items you will need to purchase during the week, so plan to have an available cash supply (no running to the ATM in the middle of the night!).

○ **Set up for the week.**

One Week After the Event

○ **Send out thank-you letters to all sponsors, donors, agencies, speakers, leaders, and volunteers.**

○ **Post pictures of camp on a church website or social networking site** (with permission—see page 127).

○ **Evaluate what happened during the week of camp (and what didn't happen)** with your design team and leaders.

○ **Begin looking for ways to continue community outreach during the months ahead.** Don't wait for next year's mission trip or camp.

Youth Program Permission Form

Event: _____

Date: _____ _____, 20 _____

Youth Name: _____

Age: _____   Grade: _____

Address: _____

_____

E-mail: _____

Parent(s) or guardian(s) name(s): _____

Parent(s) phone #: _____ (circle: home   cell   work) Txt?

Parent(s) phone #: _____ (circle: home   cell   work) Txt?

Parent(s) phone #: _____ (circle: home   cell   work) Txt?

Circle "Txt?" if a phone is able to receive text messages.

If a parent or guardian cannot be contacted, please contact:

Name: _____

Phone #: _____ (circle: home   cell   work) Txt?

Phone #: _____ (circle: home   cell   work) Txt?

Circle "Txt?" if a phone is able to receive text messages.

Allergies: _____

Other medical conditions: _____

_____

The above has my permission to participate in this event. I understand that [*church name*] _____
_____ is not liable should injury come to my child. I give my permission for emergency medical care to be given by a hospital should my child need such treatment before I am contacted.

Parent or guardian signature: _____ Date: _____

Insurance company and number: _____

Doctor's name: _____

Doctor's phone: _____

Volunteer Disclosure Form

CHURCH NAME: _____

VOLUNTEER NAME: _____

PHONE #: _____ (CIRCLE: HOME   CELL   WORK) TXT? _____

Circle "Txt?" if a phone is able to receive text messages.

ADDRESS: _____

_____

E-MAIL: _____

One mission of youth ministry is to provide safe spaces where youth can explore and affirm who they are in relationship to God and the body of Christ.

I agree to join in the fulfillment of this mission as an adult worker with youth participating in _____ Church's youth ministry activities.

The church strives to ensure the safety of all who participate in its youth ministry—both youth and adults—and thus requires disclosures from all adult workers. Any adult who wishes to help with the youth ministry should complete this form and return it to _____.

✪ As a person who will be in a position of authority within this youth ministry, I understand that I must avoid any sexual or other inappropriate contact with children, youth, and adults during and traveling to and from youth ministry events—even if someone else initiates the contact. I also understand that I should never, under any circumstances, discipline a youth or child using corporal punishment.

✪ I certify that all of the information I have provided is correct, and I understand that my participation in youth ministry activities may be prohibited if my answers are found to be inaccurate or if I am accused of abusive and/or irresponsible behavior.

✪ Exclusion from youth ministry events will continue until the completion of an official review. This review will determine whether I will be permitted to participate in future church-sponsored youth events.

HISTORY

Answer "yes" or "no." Attach an explanation for each "yes."

✪ Have you ever been convicted for a crime against a minor? _____

✪ Have you ever been convicted for the possession, use, or sale of drugs? _____

✪ Have you ever been convicted of a felony? _____

✪ Is there anything in your background that would call into question your being trusted with the supervision and care of youth, children, and/or vulnerable adults? _____

✪ Has your driver's license been suspended or revoked within the past three years? _____

✪ Has another church or a secular body ever restricted you from involvement with children, youth, or vulnerable adults? _____

Signature: _____

Date: _____

CHILD DAY CAMP REGISTRATION FORM

Dates: _____ _____, 20 _____

Child's Name: _____

AGE: _____   GRADE: _____

ADDRESS: _____

_____

PARENT(S) OR GUARDIAN(S) NAME(S): _____

PARENT(S) OR GUARDIAN(S) E-MAIL: _____

PARENT(S) PHONE #: _____ (CIRCLE: HOME   CELL   WORK) TXT?

PARENT(S) PHONE #: _____ (CIRCLE: HOME   CELL   WORK) TXT?

PARENT(S) PHONE #: _____ (CIRCLE: HOME   CELL   WORK) TXT?

Circle "Txt?" if a phone is able to receive text messages.

IF A PARENT OR GUARDIAN CANNOT BE CONTACTED, PLEASE CONTACT:

NAME: _____

PHONE #: _____ (CIRCLE: HOME   CELL   WORK) TXT?

PHONE #: _____ (CIRCLE: HOME   CELL   WORK) TXT?

Circle "Txt?" if a phone is able to receive text messages.

PARENT(S) OR GUARDIAN(S) WHO WILL PICK UP CHILD EACH DAY: _____

MAKE, MODEL, AND YEAR OF CAR: _____

OTHER ADULTS ALLOWED TO PICK UP CHILD: _____

MAKE, MODEL, AND YEAR OF CAR(S): _____

ALLERGIES: _____

OTHER MEDICAL CONDITIONS: _____

_____

The above has my permission to participate in this event. I understand that [*church name*] _____
is not liable should injury come to my child. I give my permission for emergency medical care to be given by a
hospital should my child need such treatment before I am contacted.

PARENT OR GUARDIAN SIGNATURE: _____ DATE: _____

INSURANCE COMPANY AND NUMBER: _____

DOCTOR'S NAME: _____

DOCTOR'S PHONE: _____

YOUTH MISSION CAMP REGISTRATION FORM

Date: _____ _____, 20 _____

Youth Name: _____

AGE: _____   GRADE: _____

ADDRESS: _____

_____

E-MAIL: _____

PARENT(S) OR GUARDIAN(S) NAME(S): _____

PARENT(S) PHONE #: _____ (CIRCLE: HOME   CELL   WORK) TXT?

PARENT(S) PHONE #: _____ (CIRCLE: HOME   CELL   WORK) TXT?

PARENT(S) PHONE #: _____ (CIRCLE: HOME   CELL   WORK) TXT?

Circle "Txt?" if a phone is able to receive text messages.

IF A PARENT OR GUARDIAN CANNOT BE CONTACTED, PLEASE CONTACT:

NAME: _____

PHONE #: _____ (CIRCLE: HOME   CELL   WORK) TXT?

PHONE #: _____ (CIRCLE: HOME   CELL   WORK) TXT?

Circle "Txt?" if a phone is able to receive text messages.

ALLERGIES: _____

OTHER MEDICAL CONDITIONS: _____

_____

FOOD NEEDS (VEGETARIAN, GLUTEN FREE, ETC.): _ _ _____

The above has my permission to participate in this event. I understand that [*church name*] _____
_____ is not liable should injury come to my child. I give my permission for emergency medical care to be given by a hospital should my child need such treatment before I am contacted.

PARENT OR GUARDIAN SIGNATURE: _____ DATE: _____

INSURANCE COMPANY AND NUMBER: _____

DOCTOR'S NAME: _____

DOCTOR'S PHONE: _____

SCRIPTURE INDEX

OLD TESTAMENT

NEW TESTAMENT

Preparation

- Each destination has at least one focal Scripture. Read and reflect on this Scripture ahead of time as you prepare for the destination.

- Think of the youth in your group who like to read aloud. Enlist one or two of those youth to be the Scripture readers for each activity.

Scripture Insights

REPRODUCIBLES

FOR USE WITH "ADOPT A CHILD" (SEE PAGE 9)

Thank you for allowing us to spend time with your child today. A big part of the Christmas blessing is being able to experience it through the excitement of children, and in this you have given us a blessing. We took your child shopping to purchase gifts for your family so that he or she can give gifts to family members on Christmas Day. Please try not to open these gifts until the day that you open your other Christmas gifts, since a part of the gift your child receives is the opportunity to give a gift to everyone else. Thanks again, and may you and your family truly experience God's gift that is Christmas!

FOR USE WITH "CHILDREN'S CARNIVAL" (SEE PAGE 27)

_____ has permission to use: (my child's picture, my picture)
Church name   *Circle*

in the worship service on _____.
                                                      Date

Signed: _____ Date: _____
                        Parent or Guardian

FOR USE WITH "FREE LUNCHES" (SEE PAGE 59)

Thank you for accepting this free lunch. We hope it will remind you that God's love is free to you at all times. In fact, there is nothing you can do that will take away God's love. Read Romans 8:35-39. Have a great day!

—Your Free Lunch Crew

Church: _____

Address: _____

Phone Number: _____

CPSIA information can be obtained at www.ICGtesting.com
Printed in the USA
LVOW11s1643011013

354511LV00001BC/1/P